Bob Hope's

DEAR PREZ,
I WANNA TELL YA!

A Presidential Jokebook

BY BOB HOPE
EDITED BY WARD GRANT

General Publishing Group, Inc.
Los Angeles

Publisher: W. Quay Hays
Editor: Peter Hoffman
Art Director: Maritta Tapanainen
Front cover design: Susan Anson
Cover Illustration: Dan Locke
Production Director: Trudihope Schlomowitz
New Media Director: Nadeen Torio
Color and Pre-Press Manager: Bill Castillo
Color and Pre-Press Director: Gaston Moraga
Production Assistants: Tom Archibeque, Gaspar Gonzalez

The publisher would like to thank Lorene Machado, Linda Hope and Irene Robinson.

For information:
General Publishing Group, Inc.
2701 Ocean Park Boulevard, Suite 140
Santa Monica, CA 90405

Library of Congress Cataloging-in-Publication Data

Hope, Bob, 1903-
    Dear prez, I wanna tell ya! : Bob Hope's presidential
jokebook / by Bob Hope ; edited by Ward Grant.
        p.   cm.
    ISBN 1-57544-009-1
    1. Presidents–United States–Humor.   2. American wit
and humor.   3. Political satire, American.   I. Grant, Ward.
II. Title.
E176.1.H8   1996
973'.099–dc20   96-24907
                                                      CIP

Printed in the USA by RR Donnelley & Sons Company
10 9 8 7 6 5 4 3 2 1

General Publishing Group
Los Angeles

TABLE OF CONTENTS

ACKNOWLEDGMENTS

Cover Illustration: Dan Locke, NBC Graphics, Burbank 1994

DEAR PREZ, I WANNA TELL YA! includes material from the following:

Bob Hope's Own Story: Have Tux, Will Travel as told to Pete Martin, 1954, (Simon and Schuster).

Bob Hope: A Life in Comedy by William Robert Faith, 1982, (G.P. Putnam's Sons).

The Mocking of the President by Gerald Gardner, 1988, (Wayne University Press, Detroit).

Confessions of a Hooker: My Lifelong Love Affair with Golf as told to Dwayne Netland, 1993, (Doubleday & Company).

Don't Shoot, It's Only Me by Bob Hope with Mel Shavelson, 1990, (G.P. Putnam's Sons).

SPECIAL THANKS TO:

My daughter Linda Hope for insight, encouragement and her insistence to meet the publishing deadline.

The "keepers" of the joke files: Jan Morill (now) and Marjorie Hughes (then).

The lady with the eyes and the stylebook: Suzanne Marlowe.

For help in researching things not committed to memory or the written word: Erin Coughlin, Jim Hardy, Frank Liberman, Lorene Machado, and Sue Terry.

To Ward Grant, my editor and public relations director, for helping me revisit such wonderful times.

To the group at General Publishing Group, Inc. especially

Quay Hays, Sharon Hays, editor Peter Hoffman and B. Harlan Boll, for their consideration, professionalism and patience.

And to all my writers over the years:

Jeffrey Barron
Al Boasberg
Martha Bolton
Monte Brice
Fred S. Fox
Melvin Frank
Doug Gamble
Larry Gelbart
Gig Henry
Seaman Jacobs

Milt Josefsberg
Hal Kanter
Bob Keane
Mort Lachman
Bill Larkin
Charles Lee
Wilkie Mahoney
Robert L. Mills
Norman Panama
Gene Perret

Martin Ragaway
Johnny Rapp
Sherwood Schwartz
Mel Shavelson
Raymond Siller
Charles Stewart
Norman Sullivan
Mel Tolkin
Lester White

Paul Abeyta
Howard Albrecht
Buddy Arnold
Bob Arnott
Ruth Batchlor
Harvey Berger
Bryan Blackburn
Jim Carson
Chester Castellaw
Stan Davis
Jack Donahue
Marty Farrell
Marvin Fisher
Marshall Flaum
Kathy Green
Lee Hale
Jack Haley, Jr.
Chris Hart
Stan Hart
Edmund Hartmann

Thurston Howard
Charles Isaacs
Bo Kaprall
Casey Keller
Sheldon Keller
Paul Keyes
Larry Klein
Buz Kohan
Gail Lawrence
James Lipton
Packy Markham
Larry Marks
Gordon Mitchell
Gene Moss
Ira Nickerson
Robert O'Brien
Ray Parker
Stephan Perani
Linda Perret
Pat Proft

Paul Pumpian
Larry Rhine
Peter Rich
Jack Rose
Sy Rose
Ed Scharlach
Tom Shadyac
John Shea
Ben Starr
Strawther & Williger
James Thurman
Leon Topple
Lloyd Turner
Ed Weinberger
Sol Weinstein
Harvey Weitzman
Ken & Mitzie Welch
Glenn Wheaton
Steven White

DEDICATION

To all the presidents who have extended me friendship and tolerance, who have shared a day on the golf course, a night in the White House, and an afternoon in the Rose Garden...and a lifetime of laughter.

A joke has always been a safety valve, even jokes about our presidents. Thank God they had a sense of humor or I'd probably be writing this book on Leavenworth stationery.

INTRODUCTION

B ob credits Will Rogers with being the seminal political humorist. He's right. I recall a story about Will Rogers and President Calvin Coolidge, who reportedly lacked a sense of humor. Someone bet Rogers he couldn't make Coolidge laugh. During a reception at the White House, Rogers was introduced to the President. Will, it was reported, leaned close to Coolidge and said, "I'm sorry, I didn't get the name." Rogers won the bet.

I hope that story is true because it's the perfect example of what political humor is all about. Politicians, especially presidents, become insulated from the day-to-day activities of ordinary citizens and some (no names here) behave as if they've undergone a coronation rather than an election.

It's the job of the comedian to remind presidents that they are just temporary residents of the White House, and eventually they will have to return to the real world.

Bob's political humor has never been mean-spirited or unfair. He needles Republicans and Democrats with equal fervor. And young comedians who read this book will realize that you can get laughs without being vicious or foul-mouthed.

This is not only a funny book, but a historical perspective of what was happening in our country. So thank you, Bob, not only for the laughs, but for some pleasant reminders of how things were.

Johnny Carson

Where else but in America...

PROLOGUE

Hoover and BH (Before Hoover)

No one party can fool all of the people all of the time; that's why we have two parties.

PEOPLE HAVE BEEN MAKING FUN of their government leaders since the pharaohs of Egypt started playing with blocks. True, early political commentators didn't live long, but they still provided a good laugh or two on the way to the gallows, the tower, the henchman...whoever the critics were at the time.

Kings and queens always had their fools. The czar of Russia had his three stooges, Curly, Moe and Rasputin (they preceded the Marx Brothers) and all our presidents had Congress.

Way back in America's history, journalists, political activists and cartoonists were the primary critics of our country's leaders. There may be others more well known, but for me, Will Rogers, with his down-home way, made ridiculing political leaders an art form. And that art form has been embraced by America's humorists ever since.

Contrary to rumors, I did not entertain the troops at Valley

Forge with jokes about George Washington. Not that there wasn't a lot of material—his wooden teeth, standing up in boats—and if he slept at all the places they say he did, no wonder they called him the "Father of our Country."

But the truth is, I have been poking fun at our presidents for a long time. I don't know exactly who was in office when I started, but he was wearing a coonskin cap. (And I've only had my taxes audited five times.)

The first presidential joke I ever told was about George Washington:

George told his father, "I cannot tell a lie." I don't know how he made it in politics!

And speaking of George, I've had a lot of fun with him over the years:

George Washington said, "Father, I cannot tell a lie"—a quality that helped get him into the Oval Office but kept him off the golf course.

He was our only president who left his teeth in a glass of varnish at night.

And one that never fails at a personal appearance:

A youngster in a prankish mood tossed the family outhouse over an embankment. His father was furious and asked who did it. The kid remembered the story of George Washington chopping down the cherry tree and said, "Father, I cannot tell a lie. I did it." Whereupon his father gave him the thrashing of his life.

The poor kid said, "How come when George Washington said that, his father didn't punish him?" The man replied, "George Washington's father wasn't sitting in the cherry tree at the time."

My first presidential joke about a president in office was about Herbert Hoover. I also think he was the first president I voted for…or against (I can't remember which). Hoover was running for re-election and trying to run even harder to get away from the nation's Great Depression. His campaign slogan was "Prosperity is just around the corner." I was in vaudeville at the Orpheum in New York. In the "afterpiece" ("Antics of 1930") I combined what was then considered taboo—politics and bathroom humor:

> *Isn't this some theater? I was standing out in front watching the other acts when a lady rushed up to me and said, "Pardon me, young man, can you help me find the rest room?"*

> *And I said, "Yes, ma'am, it's just around the corner." And she said, "Don't give me any of that Hoover talk, I've got to go."*

> *Hoover also promised the nation "a car in every garage and a chicken in every pot." Today, he'd have to replace "garage" and "pot" with underground parking and a microwave.*

Playing on the words and deeds of presidents for whom I was not old enough to vote has become a fun pastime for my writers and for me:

> *I've always felt close to Calvin Coolidge—"Silent Cal."*

> *…He was named after one of my audiences.*

> *…I don't know who moved his eyes and did the voice.*

"Silent Cal" was the first president to deliver a State of the Union address in sign language.

> *…He made Jimmy Stewart sound like Howard Cosell.*

> *…He also was reported to have said, "If you never say anything, you won't be called upon to repeat it."*

Thomas Jefferson called the presidency "splendid misery." "Splendid misery"—that's like watching your mother-in-law drive off a cliff in your new Chrysler. (Since I was being sponsored by Chrysler Motors when I said that, it was a laugh and a commercial at the same time.)

… "Splendid misery"—that's the same thing I call my golf game.

Jefferson also said, "Never spend your money before you have it." That's one presidential quote my wife, Dolores, never heard.

Teddy Roosevelt said, "Speak softly and carry a big stick," which just means…if you're going to host a talk show, watch out for flying chairs.

That was before the presidents had dogs. Now their motto is "Walk softly and carry a pooper-scooper."

Times have changed. In L.A. now, our motto is "Walk softly and carry a pit bull."

About Abraham Lincoln:

Lincoln said, "You can fool all of the people some of the time and some of the people all of the time, but you can't fool all of the people all of the time." Abe made that statement right after he'd seen my act.

…Thank God none of my agents ever believed him.

"Honest Abe"…his parents named him that. They figured he could always make a living as a used-car salesman.

Everyone knows about Ulysses S. Grant:

He drank so much he made Dean Martin look like part of the Pepsi Generation.

When Grant was president, they played "Hail to the Chief" to the tune of "Melancholy Baby."

Two jokes that I recycle every chance I get followed the first time I stayed at the White House at the invitation of Ike and Mamie Eisenhower. They put me up in the Lincoln Room…

…The next morning I woke up and freed my writers.

…But all through the night I kept hearing a voice asking, "How did the play end?"

Vice presidents, presidential hopefuls and many of our past presidents, for the most part, don't rank high in the public's mind. I once had a joke about Henry Clay:

Henry Clay said, "I would rather be right than president."

And a heckler in the audience yelled out, "Who's Henry Clay?" I yelled back, "He was with the Whig Party and nearly defeated James Polk." "Who's James Polk?" I never finished the joke.

Being the president of the United States is a rough job, but somebody's got to do it! Not me. Believe it or not, I was asked twice about running for the office. Once was for real. After I picked myself up off the floor from laughing, they told me they were serious.

I said, "I am deeply honored but first of all, I don't qualify—I was born in England."

"We can fix that," they said.

To bring them to their senses I tried some humor. "I can't take the cut in salary and Dolores will refuse to move into a smaller house.…Me, run a nation? I haven't figured out daylight-saving yet.…Besides, aren't there enough comedians in Washington already?"

The other time was for fun. It was in 1967. Lyndon Johnson was the president and I was the guest of honor at the National Press Club's annual Alfalfa Club dinner. Since the club's inception, the plan for the evening has been for the chairman to announce that the dinner is adjourned and the convention of the Alfalfa Party is convened. A resolution is then read nominating their honored guest as president of the United States on the Alfalfa ticket. I was the honored guest. I ran on the Humor ticket. Here's some of my acceptance speech:

It's exciting just thinking about being president for four years. I've never had a sponsor that long.

I'm not one of those candidates who is afraid to take a stand on controversial issues. Let it be noted in the record that I am in favor of motherhood and against the tsetse fly.

However, I am not as courageous and forthright as the incumbent....I'm afraid to come out 100 percent against poverty....I say, let's wait till we hear their side of it.

The war on poverty was so successful that Lyndon's next move will be a war on wealth. He's gonna give rich people something they've never had—poverty.

First thing I'll do is lower the voting age to 17, to include Tuesday Weld. Who knows? If we let her in our party, maybe she'll invite us to hers.

And I won't have any trouble working with Congress. I get along well with other comedians.

I'm not a Republican or Democrat...Neither a liberal nor a conservative....I'm just a middle-of-the-road monologist who believes in the patriotic precept that what's good for my ratings is good for my country.

As for my Cabinet:

I'll have Jayne Mansfield for my running mate. I'm sure she'll measure up.

I'll name Zsa Zsa Gabor to head our Bureau of Wildlife.

My wife, Dolores, for secretary of state....She'd be great with foreign negotiations. She can spot a lie before I get it out of my mouth.

For secretary of defense: John Wayne. He can win wars by himself without getting any of the rest of us involved.

Raquel Welch in charge of domestic affairs....Let's see Congress veto that!

I have a few ideas for ambassadorships. Milton Berle is going to love it on Devil's Island.

But, seriously, I'm lucky. I've known 11 presidents about as intimately as a man can without being either a fellow politician or related. I've golfed with them, dined with them, told jokes with them. I've even had them steal my material.

Laughter is nonpartisan—a great leveler. And maybe that's the one thing all 11 presidents have in common. As long as it's funny, you can say almost anything to them and get away with it.

For Bob Hope from his friend
Franklin D Roosevelt

FRANKLIN DELANO ROOSEVELT

*Roosevelt was the first president I met personally.
The rest told me to mail my taxes in.*

FDR WAS A RICH MAN'S SON who had been governor of New York. In 1921 he fell victim to polio, which kept him confined to a wheelchair for the rest of his life. With his famous grin and tilted cigarette holder, he chose to ignore his disability. So, amazingly, did the press. I checked my files, and neither I nor anyone else ever mentioned his wheelchair. The depression and his promise to repeal Prohibition ensured his election over incumbent Herbert Hoover.

In 1940 he was re-elected for an unprecedented third term, beating his Republican opponent, Wendell L. Willkie, a former utilities company president. (I still have a "Win with Willkie" button somewhere in the desk drawer of my old office.) The campaign was a vocal one, utilizing national radio as the political soapbox, which prompted this opening remark on one of my radio shows:

I want to thank both political candidates for giving up their time so this program can be heard.

In December 1941 we were at war. Roosevelt told the nation that we "had nothing to fear but fear itself" and we believed him. He was our commander in chief. He was our country. What's more, he was the greatest audience I ever worked for.

My biggest thrill was to receive an invitation to appear in Washington and entertain Roosevelt at the White House Correspondents' dinner. This was in 1943, when the United States was in the war all the way. Roosevelt had the affection of the whole nation, not only because of the way he was handling the war, but because we all knew that his wife, Eleanor, was always flying all over the world on some mission or other. Our show was playing an Army camp in Mobile, Alabama, when I got the invitation. I was a little nervous and tried to get out of it by saying I couldn't get airplane reservations. Well, FDR fixed that. He had General Hap Arnold sandwich me onto an Air Force plane. I had to go. It was my first flight as a ham sandwich.

The dinner was held in the ballroom of the Statler Hotel. There were some 800 correspondents, government officials, ambassadors and other VIPs in the audience... *and* Franklin Delano Roosevelt. I arrived late. (When I was preparing to do the show, someone asked me if I ever got nervous facing a large audience. I said, "All the time— until I hear that first laugh.") As I looked at the president, seated on a raised dais at the side of the ballroom where everyone could watch him, I saw all the cares of wartime written on his lined face. I didn't think I was ever going to

What a pleasure meeting First Lady Eleanor Roosevelt...thankfully, she didn't hold a grudge for some of my one-liners at her expense. It was a Washington D.C. event during World War II. That's Vice President Henry A. Wallace seated at the table with her. The men standing were major politicians...or waiters.

hear a laugh. But I was never accused of being bashful, so I plunged right in:

> *Good evening, Mr. President. I heard you just had a conference with Winston Churchill on a battleship about war strategy. War strategy, meaning, "Where will we attack the enemy and how are we going to keep Eleanor out of the crossfire?"*

All eyes were glued on FDR, waiting for his reaction before anybody dared crack a smile. I thought, *Uh-oh, I've had it.* Well, he suddenly threw his head back and roared with laugher. The place exploded and I was saved. He laughed so loud that I wanted to sign him up for my studio audience.

One of Roosevelt's greatest critics was Colonel Bertie McCormick, the powerful publisher of the *Chicago Tribune*, which printed daily editorials attacking FDR. Roosevelt had a Scottie dog named Fala, so I said:

Fala was the only canine in history to be house-broken on the Tribune.

The president laughed so hard that he almost swallowed his cigarette holder. I followed that with another reference to the fact that Franklin's wife was never home and said that he was the first president in history who ate out. FDR slapped the table and laughed so hard I almost voted Democratic.

However, this was not my first time in the Roosevelt environment. I was a mere child at the time (that's just under 40) when I attended a White House lawn party as a guest (me and half of Hollywood) of First Lady Eleanor Roosevelt.

The occasion was the reception for the Victory Caravan, a special train carrying some of the nation's most popular entertainers across the country, rehearsing along the way, for the kickoff of a two-week whistle-stop tour for the Army and Navy Relief Funds. At the party some of the stars who performed for Mrs. Roosevelt were Charles Boyer, James Cagney, Cary Grant, Bing Crosby, Laurel and Hardy, Groucho Marx and a wonderful musical-comedy star, Charlotte Greenwood, who was famous as a high kicker, her long legs extending way over her pretty head. As Charlotte was dancing, Groucho leaned over to Mrs. Roosevelt and said,

"You know, with a little practice, you could do that, too."

It was Roosevelt who really got me into the spirit of poking fun at presidents. I learned I had to work on making an insult humorous so as to only dent the presidential ego, not damage it; to give equal insult time to the leadership of both political parties; and to try to be sensitive to crucial "tender spots." I've always had great respect for the office of the president of the United States and for the men who have accepted its challenges.

Roosevelt became famous for his fireside chats on the radio.

I was with Roosevelt during one of his famous fireside chats. He turned to me and said, "Put another log on the fire, boy."

(Today's version)

Everyone would gather around their radios to listen to FDR's fireside chats. Imagine, listening to someone on the radio besides a tiny little German woman talking about sex.

During World War II, "rationing" was one of the battles we faced on the home front. Everyone, including the politicians, was affected.

(Radio show, June 2, 1942)

With rationing, the Republican Party had to change their mascot to a gopher and the Democratic donkey had to go on the nine-day diet. It's the first time any Democrat has been on a diet since the Hoover administration.

(*Radio show, October 6, 1942*)

*You know, President Roosevelt paid a visit to
San Francisco last week. And you should see the
way the president's car was closely guarded.
There were eight Secret Service men around it—
two for each tire.*

It was President Roosevelt who first asked me to entertain the troops overseas:

*He asked me because he said I was popular, talented
and expendable.*

*...I asked him, "Where should I go, sir?" He
answered, "I don't know—just follow Eleanor."*

*You know how soldiers raise their fingers in a "V"
for victory when President Roosevelt passes? Well,
when I pass, they use 'em for slingshots.*

On the crowded conditions in our nation's capital:

*There's really a shortage of hotel rooms in
Washington. I even saw a Democrat sleeping in
the park.*

*Imagine, Roosevelt and Churchill meeting in Africa.
Just shows you how crowded the Washington hotels
must be.*

*Following Africa, Roosevelt flew to Brazil. What
some people won't do to get a second cup of coffee.*

On Roosevelt being elected to a fourth term in office:

Or as the Republicans refer to those years...Oops!

One more time for Eleanor (dinner honoring General Omar Bradley in Washington, D.C., May 30, 1961):

It's always a pleasure to see Mrs. Roosevelt and Congressman Roosevelt. So many Roosevelts and Kennedys. There's one thing you have to say about the Democrats: They don't depend on recruiting.

You all know Mrs. Roosevelt. She originated the "Go Now, Go Again Later" plan.

She was a little late arriving here tonight....She couldn't get anyone to park her tractor.

On White House security:

It's pretty tough to get into the White House these days. Fala meets you at the front door and sniffs you. If you're a Democrat he lets you get to your seat and if you're a Republican you go in without one.

Updates of Roosevelt's famous quote, "We have nothing to fear but fear itself":

Obviously, he never heard about ratings.

...Or played golf with Jerry Ford.

These are the words my dentist has printed on his ceiling while he's doing root canals.

On my radio show, April 17, 1945, after FDR's death, I replaced my monologue with:

A few seconds ago we listened to the voice of Harry S. Truman, the 33rd president of the United States of America. You know, we lost a man who didn't need jokes to make laughter a part of American life. He had a little formula for humor all his own. You've heard of it—they call it the Four Freedoms. One of these is Freedom from Fear. Yessir, one of FDR's ideas must have been that people who have no fear are not afraid to laugh. Not much like Poland under Germany, is it? Incidentally, our gang will never forget the few times that we were doing our stuff in our nation's capital, and we'd hear Mr. Roosevelt laugh. It was a wonderful laugh. And when he smiled, he smiled out loud. Like as not, the gag was one about Eleanor and her habit of getting around the world as though the world was the backyard at Hyde Park. And we'd just like to say this tonight: When you're reserving a space in your heart for FDR, a great man, leave a little for a great lady, too.

HARRY S. TRUMAN

Congress—that's "People Are Funny" with your money. I don't want you to think I'm knocking Congress. I'm not. All I know is they just spend it faster than I can make it.

TRUMAN WAS A HABERDASHER in Independence, Missouri, before he was elected to the Senate. He was small in stature, played "The Missouri Waltz" on the piano, and his daughter wanted to be an opera singer. This was the stuff from which great one-liners are made. For FDR's third term, he chose Truman to be his vice presidential running mate.

In 1944 I was at the White House for a photo session for a war bond relief drive. I was posing with Mrs. Roosevelt and Edward Stettinius, the secretary of state. I was more than a little annoyed at this other person who kept trying to get into the shots. Then Stettinius said, "Oh,

1951. President Truman, just before he sat down at the piano.

Bob, do you know the vice president?"

I said, "I'm sorry, Mr. Truman. I didn't recognize you." Truman said, "That's the best part of this job."

Truman was seemingly a mild man, but when Roosevelt passed away early in his fourth term, Harry took the reins of the presidency firmly in his hands. He had a little sign on his desk in the Oval Office that read THE BUCK STOPS HERE—and he meant it. He wouldn't be pushed around by anybody...like when deciding to drop the atomic bomb, or ousting General Douglas MacArthur for ignoring presidential orders in Korea, or verbally taking to task that music critic who dared to suggest that daughter Margaret couldn't sing. All of which prompted me to openly comment:

> *[Truman] rules the country with an iron fist...the same way he plays the piano.*

Columnist Drew Pearson, who had seconded the music critic's motion, bugged him even worse. "Bob," Truman told me, "if it wasn't for that S.O.B. across the Potomac, I'd really love being president."

For the 1948 presidential race, the Democrats had no other choice but to nominate Truman. His running mate was Alben W. Barkley and his Republican opponent was the governor of New York, Thomas E. Dewey. The press, the pollsters, politicians on both sides of the aisle, and even Truman himself expected Truman to lose. The *Chicago Tribune* was so sure of it that their one-line headline on election night read: DEWEY DEFEATS TRUMAN.

On that famous morning in November 1948, after Truman was elected and Tom Dewey wasn't, I happened to get the news early that Dewey had unexpectedly conceded to Truman. I rushed to Western Union and whipped off a one-word congratulatory telegram to the White House: "Unpack." Harry never forgot it—he put it under the glass on his desk and pointed it out to visitors.

Speaking of Truman and White House visitors, I was doing my radio show in D.C. when I got a call from Truman inviting me to dinner at the White House. I had to send my regrets because I didn't want to leave my cast members, but I offered to bring Jerry Colonna and Vera Vague over after the broadcast and do a show for him, his family and his staff. He accepted the idea and after the show he took me aside and said: "Once a year, members of Congress come over and we give them a tour of the White House." He patted me on the shoulder and whispered, "Come on, I'll show you how we do it." And he did. I got a personal tour of the White House by the resident president.

I liked Harry. He always said exactly what he thought. When he was in the Senate, he became known as "Give-'Em-Hell Harry," and when he was president, he was great copy. Unfortunately, most of it was unprintable. The most famous Truman story was from his wife, Bess. She said:

> *Harry made a speech at the Washington Garden Club and kept referring to "the good manure" that must be used on flowers. Some society woman complained to me, "Bess, couldn't you get the president to say 'fertilizer'?" And I said, "Heavens no. It took me 25 years to get him to say 'manure.'"*

President Truman, through Stuart Symington (friend, former senator and then secretary of the Air Force), asked Dolores and me to participate in the Berlin Airlift, Christmas 1948. I guess he figured we needed a chaperon and that he could do without his vice president for a while because he sent Alben Barkley on the trip with us. Hard as I tried, I just couldn't get Barkley to be my straight man.

Just prior to the 1952 presidential campaign I made reference to Truman's uphill battle against Dwight D. Eisenhower. My Chesterfield radio monologue, delivered just after Princess Elizabeth and Prince Philip had visited Washington, went something like this:

> *...Then Elizabeth asked Margaret Truman what a Republican was and Margaret said, "I don't know. Every time the subject comes up my parents make me leave the room."...But they had a nice visit, and when the princess left the White House, she said, "I hope to be back next year, Mr. President," and President Truman said, "Me, too."*

Even in retirement Truman was always good subject matter for humor. He personally liked the one from my TV special from New York in November 1953:

Ex-President Hoover lives on the floor above the Trumans. It's a little embarrassing for the management. Every night Hoover pounds on the steam pipes and shouts, "Stop with that piano playing down there!" And Mr. Truman shouts back, "Don't pick on me. I couldn't afford lessons until you were out of office."

A Sampling of the "Give 'em Hell Harry" Years

Truman/Dewey race for the White House:

This campaign promises to be a hot battle. Truman has announced that he's not going to leave the White House, and Dewey says he's moving in. That'll be a nice situation....I can just see the towels in the White House bathroom...Marked "his" and "his."

Yessir, the Democrats did so well in the election, they're even coming out with a few new products named after the president....They've got a thing called the "Harry Truman popsicle"—it's a frozen Republican on a stick.

Race for the presidency Truman vs. Eisenhower vs. Senator Taft:

Presidential elections are shaping up pretty well. Truman is singing "Just One More Chance," Taft is singing "I Get Ideas" and Eisenhower is whistling "In the Cool, Cool, Cool of the Evening, Tell Them I'll Be There."

Post–World War II relationships:

Now that the war is over, England needs money. When Truman met Winston Churchill he said to Winston, "You look like a million dollars." And Churchill replied, "That'll do for a down payment."…Churchill brought Truman a present all the way from England, and Harry wanted to give him something to take back, but Eisenhower wouldn't fit in his suitcase.

Truman was a haberdasher…

…Which frightened a lot of people. Never trust a politician who knows how to measure your inseam.

…He could shake your hand and measure you for a suit at the same time.

It's true, he was a haberdasher by trade. If it wasn't for him, the suit on the Lincoln Memorial never would have fit.

He made great suits. But if he knew you were a Republican, it wasn't wise to let him measure your inseam.

Of Margaret's singing:

Truman tried to be nice about his daughter's singing. I was there the day Margaret found out her father didn't wear earmuffs because of the cold.

Best wishes to the greatest of pretenders us from
Harry Truman

*He once wrote a nasty letter to a music critic who
had given his daughter a bad review. It helps to
have a father who's tone deaf.*

*Harry didn't care about image. That's because
he had a weapon that could bring the world to its
knees—Margaret Truman's singing.*

I once sat at the piano with Harry Truman as he played
"The Missouri Waltz."

(1987 TV monologue)

*Then there was Harry Truman—the Liberace of the
liberals. Everyone laughed at Truman and his piano
but little do they know that it was because of his
playing that his neighbors first sent him to Congress.*

Where else but in America can you do a "drop in" on an ex-president and first lady? Here I stand with Bess and Harry Truman on the porch of their home in Independence, Missouri, several years after he left office.

Even his famous quotes were fair game:

"The White House is the finest prison in the world."... I guess they make license plates in the Lincoln Bedroom.

"If you can't stand the heat, get out of the kitchen." The same thing was once said to me by Julia Child.

Quite a few years after Truman left office I was in Kansas City, Missouri (with Disney for Eisenhower's "People to People" event), when the former president's red-haired aide approached me after the show and said, "The president and Mrs. Truman would like you to drop in to see them after the show. The president said you were an Independent, so I guess it's all right." I took the short trip to Independence and visited with the Trumans on the front porch of their charming little home. As I left, Truman shook my hand and said, "Drop in anytime, will ya?" I got the feeling that he was lonesome.

DWIGHT DAVID EISENHOWER

*Over the years, I've played golf with a lot of
presidents, although not all of them play.
Historically, most of the real swingers have
been in Congress.*

ONE OF THE GREATEST MOMENTS of my life
was meeting General Dwight David Eisenhower in Algiers
in 1943. That was before he became famous for his golf
game and painting and as president of Columbia
University. Oh, and as president of the United States, too.

It was during World War II. My little band of gypsies
and I were on a North African GI tour doing three or four
shows a day for our servicemen and women serving in
Sicily and Tunisia and were heading for Algiers to broadcast a show to the United States. During rehearsal we
received word that General Eisenhower would like to
meet us at his headquarters. His account of the story,

strangely enough, agrees with mine. The following excerpt is from his letter, to be read at a USO dinner I was attending:

> *...Once, after Bob and his company had been subject to a bombing raid in the town of Bizerte [Tunisia], he came back to Algiers where I promised him a night of peace and rest. Imagine my embarrassment when, on that very night, we had a raid on Algiers and Bob had to resign himself to a couple of hours in a dark wine cellar.*

One of the greatest moments of my life was meeting General Dwight D. Eisenhower in Tunis (1943). This was before he became famous for his golf game.

I feel like a worn cloth bookmark at the Desert Classic in between two national heroes—baseball great Sandy Koufax and President Eisenhower.

The wine cellar didn't bother me. It was all that other stuff flying overhead that bothered me. He told me in no uncertain terms, "You're perfectly safe here. We're too strong for them. They can't get in." Contrary to what we've all been told, generals can be wrong.

Speculation that Eisenhower would run for president in 1952 was high, but Ike was hesitant about any such commitment; a fact worthy of a couple of mentions in my concert monologues early in the year:

> *...Eisenhower says he'll run if he's drafted. The last guy who ran when he was drafted is doing five to ten on Alcatraz.*

> *...You can't blame Eisenhower for refusing to be a candidate. After being a general so long, he doesn't like the idea of being back in a regiment.*

Eisenhower and New York Governor Nelson Rockefeller showing off their trophies. This was before Rockefeller became an "unknown" as vice president.

But a major part of the American public encouraged the reluctant candidate to run for office; he was a real live hero and a Republican. I had to comment in my April and June 1952 monologues:

> *...Everybody's excited about General Eisenhower running for president. Of course, being a busy general, he'll probably have a staff sergeant run for him. And I happen to know why he's running for president. It's the only way he can get out of the Army.*

> *...Eisenhower said that if he was elected, he was going to give General Douglas MacArthur a very important job. Do you think we need an ambassador at the North Pole?*

...Eisenhower hasn't done any campaigning yet but he no longer calls the soldiers "GIs"—now he just says, "Fellow voters."

Truman had decided not to run and the Democratic nominee became Illinois governor and super-intellectual Adlai E. Stevenson (grandson of A.E. Stevenson, vice president under Grover Cleveland. Then again, a vice president, who remembers?). But Stevenson and Republican hopeful Howard Taft were no match for Eisenhower. The whole nation was rallying behind the campaign slogan "I Like Ike." I had a problem. I liked Ike, too...and this was the year I really had to be non-partisan. NBC had asked me to be one of their news commentators at both conventions.

However, on my first Colgate Comedy Hour of the new NBC season I devoted the entire monologue to politics:

...I want to thank all the candidates for giving up this time to make room for another comedian....
I'm so confused, I don't know whether to join the Democrats who are voting for Eisenhower, or the Democrats who are voting for Stevenson...or [Bing] Crosby, who's still voting for John Quincy Adams.... This election will make history. It's the first time a general waits for the troops to make the decision.... Both parties are after the farm votes. They've made so many speeches, the farmers expect the biggest crops of their lives.

...Truman is not happy with all the Republican visitors to the White House. They keep bringing their suitcases.

A month before taking office, Eisenhower kept one of his campaign promises—to visit Korea in an effort to end the war there. (Many were hopeful at the time that this would develop a new trend in presidential campaigning. Not!) What was even more surprising was that the whole matter was kept a secret until he had returned to the States. I joked in concert:

> *...I was curious so I called the Pentagon and said, "Tell me, how'd you manage to sneak Eisenhower out of the country without a soul knowing about it?" And they said, "Never mind how we did it.... But we'll be happy to do the same for you sometime."*

> *...And the general himself was really secretive.... He registered at the hotel in Tokyo as John Smith and friend—at least they think it was the general.*

Finally, a golfer in the White House. Eisenhower won by a landslide. His vice president was Richard Milhous Nixon. I had some fun with the inauguration on my February special:

> *...After the swearing-in ceremonies, 50,000 Republicans paraded through the streets of Washington for three hours—nobody could remember how to get to the Capitol....And you could tell which were the Republicans and which were the Democrats at the inauguration—the Republicans were facing the platform.*

> *...They had a lot of musical talent at the inauguration. They wanted to invite Jose Iturbi, but Ike was against it. He said, "The last time we had a piano player in Washington, he stayed for eight years!"*

Frances Langford renews aquaintance with President Eisenhower at the Desert Classic in Palm Springs.

The two dominant, and constant, humor themes for Eisenhower were:

the president as a warrior...

Ike's election has created a new slogan, "Join the Army and see the White House."...Having a general for president is gonna be something—I can't wait till he puts Congress on KP.

At his first formal White House dinner, he made Mamie serve pheasant on a shingle.

...and the president as a golfer.

First Lady Mamie Eisenhower is having trouble with Ike and his golf game at the White House. Not only does he wear his golf shoes in the living quarters but he doesn't replace his divots in the carpet.

One of the most memorable times was the round of golf I played with Ike in 1953 at Burning Tree. The president, Senator Prescott Bush (George's father), Stuart Symington (then senator from Missouri) and I made up the foursome. Ike and I were partners. I asked, "What do you want to bet?"

"I usually play for a dollar, dollar, dollar," Ike said. (This means that a dollar is wagered on the first nine, another on the second nine and another on all eighteen.) "Funny thing," Ike went on. "I've just lent a million and a half dollars to Bolivia, and here I am playing for a dollar, dollar, dollar."

The following night at the White House Correspondents' Association annual banquet, Ike was a willing target:

I knew the president when he was a general and really had power....I played golf with him yesterday. It's hard to beat a guy who rattles his medals while you're putting....Ike uses a short Democrat for a tee.

On my next telecast I told the audience:

I had the pleasure of playing golf with the president the other day...and I'd like to go on record right now by saying that if he slices the budget like he slices a ball, the nation has nothing to worry about.

Underneath my sweater I'm still wearing my "I Like Ike" button.

In 1956, Ike was at the peak of his popularity, so his rematch with Adlai Stevenson was rather lopsided. Ike won by an electoral vote of 437 to 73. The campaign was as exciting as sitting around watching concrete harden. The only humorous highlight came from Stevenson's running mate, Tennessee Senator Estes Kefauver, who insisted on wearing a coonskin cap throughout the campaign.

I personally knew both Ike and Adlai, but I knew Ike better because we played golf together. And I could say things like, "Ike is all Army. He loves golf, but if you lose, you not only have to pay him, he makes you eat K-rations. And sometimes, Ike cooks. I once played nine holes with one of his meatballs."

I just could not deal directly with Eisenhower's heart attack in 1955 but I had fun from the stage with his recovery and his time away from the White House:

> *Ike has taken up painting now instead of playing golf. It's fewer strokes....As a painter he's ahead of his time—we won't have apples that shape for a hundred years, at least.*

Ike at the Classic Ball in Palm Springs. You're looking at Vic Damone, Jane Powell and Pearl Bailey.

Even my affectionate goodbye as he stepped down as chief executive was about golf:

You remember Ike—he was the pro in the White House....He'll have a lot of time to play golf—the unemployment office doesn't have many jobs in his category....But I hope he enjoys himself.

He did and so did I. We spent many wonderful hours in Palm Springs on the golf course and planning the Eisenhower Medical Center there.

Even Irving Berlin wrote a song, "We Like Ike."

Eisenhower sent me a letter saying that he appreciated knowing me. He wrote, "My parents started out their married life in 1885 in the town of Hope, Kansas. Throughout my life the association of the names of Hope and Eisenhower has had a subconscious appeal."

Ike's parents, David Jacob and Elizabeth Stover, moved from Kansas to Texas, where he and his brother, Milton, were born and brought up. Milton, by the way, served as president at three major universities. My favorite true story about Dwight and his mother:

Ike had a ticker-tape parade in Manhattan after V-E Day. Seated in an open car in the parade was his mother. "You must be very proud of your son," enthused a newspaperwoman. "Which one?" replied Mrs. Eisenhower.

Goodwill tour to South America:

Nixon briefed him on South America—but he's going anyway.

Ike and Mamie loved Palm Springs....And the nation loved them. It was always an honor to have them attend the Desert Classic.

Ike's not afraid. He's been through two wars and Ladies' Day at the Gettysburg Country Club.

Actually, when he got to the airport he told the pilot, "Take me anywhere. We've got trouble all over."

Moving into the White House:

I wouldn't say the White House was booby-trapped, but the general's bed was short-sheeted, there was salt in the sugar bowl and all the doors to the washrooms were marked, "Enlisted Personnel Only."

President Truman said he wouldn't say anything bad about President Eisenhower, but someone better get to Ike and tell him not to comment about Margaret's singing.

Ike wins a second term as president:

Mamie is really relieved that Ike has another four years in the White House. She hasn't had time to clean up the spike marks in the hallway.

The inauguration was televised and one Democrat was complaining about it. He said, "That's the trouble with television—too many reruns."

The guests at the inaugural dinner consumed a terrific amount of food—3,000 steaks, 1,000 hamburgers, 200 turkeys...and Lawrence Welk's drummer is missing.

Did you see President Eisenhower's press conference on TV? I thought Ike was very good, although he could use a little coaching. A couple of times there he was smiling at Democrats.

The president's press conference got a wonderful review in **Variety.** *It said, "Prez Smash at News Bash. Ike No Rube on Tube."*

"Grandpa Moses":

Ike is really quite a good painter. In fact, I hear that every time he goes out to play golf, Grandma Moses heaves a sigh of relief.

I think it's wonderful that Ike paints; it's relaxing and besides, a guy without a steady job should always have something to fall back on.

Even Ike had budget problems:

Ike delivered his budget economy message to Congress and immediately set about practicing what he preached. The last I heard, they were taking in boarders at the White House. They even tried to rent Harry his old room back.

...But Ike has a wonderful idea for balancing the budget: Now it's just a question of what kind of hotel Conrad Hilton can make out of the Pentagon.

The Eisenhowers depart the White House:

Ike and Mamie are leaving the White House. Moving is quite a problem. They're trying to figure out how to get all their furniture in a golf cart.

It will be a sad day for the neighbors on Pennsylvania Avenue. They'll have to start buying their own golf balls.

Ike's had a few surprises on the golf course lately. Now he's starting to find out who he really can beat.

Of course, everyone's wondering what Ike is going to do after he leaves the presidency—he's too old to re-enlist.

JOHN FITZGERALD KENNEDY

When I meet a president for the first time, I always ask how I can get that sort of power, prestige and respect. He always asks me how he can get residuals.

JUST WHO WAS THIS YOUNG, unknown Bostonian who took the American public by storm when he became the 35th president of the United States by defeating a man with an international image who served as vice president for eight years? The fact that he was the son of an influential ambassador and financier, a Harvard graduate, a Navy hero, a congressman (D-Massachusetts) at the age of 30 and a senator at 35 helped. He also had written a best-selling book. But "Jack" Kennedy was relatively unknown outside his home state and Washington, D.C. He was a Roman Catholic and not knowledgeable in foreign affairs. How'd he reach such heights so fast? Well, he

President Kennedy had told me to invite the family and some friends—so I did. Left to right: you know who, Dolores, JFK, daughters Linda and Nora and sons Tony and Kelly, and Stuart Symington.

was sophisticated and had a quick wit, intelligence, an infectious smile and a great head of hair. And as I indicated in a monologue in the spring of 1960, he had money:

I must say the senator's victory in Wisconsin was a triumph for democracy. It proves that a millionaire has just as good a chance as anybody else.

Here was a man with all the trappings of a King Arthur: a beautiful wife of great breeding and taste; two adorable children; and an extended family of wealth, influence and some mystery. (No wonder they called the Kennedy White House "Camelot.") But most of all, this young man had charisma and a wonderful sense of humor. All this worked in his favor as he got national attention in the televised Nixon/Kennedy debates.

The television season and the political season started about the same time, so there was plenty of comedy material. I opened my first show saying:

Here I am, starting another season in television.
What else can I do? I'm too old to be a candidate....
A few months ago Kennedy's mother said, "You have
a choice. Do you want to go to camp this year or run
for president?"

I like giving youth a chance, but do we really want
a president who rides for half fare on the bus?

The 1960 presidential campaign came to a climax with
the TV debates between the candidates. Lighting and
makeup may have been the deciding factor in a close
race—Kennedy won by .3 percent. And, seemingly, before
the last vote was counted, he had presented the names for
his young Cabinet, including his brother Bobby as attorney general. I shared the dais with JFK at the Alfalfa Club
dinner in February 1961, and couldn't resist:

President Kennedy has picked pretty good help—
Harvard is emptier than our Treasury. There are
so many professors in the Cabinet that you can't
leave the White House without raising your
hand....The attorney general was 20 minutes late
for a meeting this morning and he had to bring a
note from his mother.

At his turn at the podium, Kennedy feigned surprise
that anyone would object to his nominating his brother as
attorney general: "What's wrong with his getting a little
legal experience before he goes into business for himself?"
What set Kennedy apart from all other presidents was
his ability to genuinely laugh at himself. He opened the
floodgates for presidential humor, the likes of which had
never been seen before. He enjoyed the ribbing and gave

as good as he got. He could ad-lib with you on equal terms. Not just with me, but everybody. No topic seemed sacred—his family, his rocking chair, his foreign policy....

(TV monologue, April 1961)

A few months ago, who'd have thought Ike would be a full general again and Kennedy would be singing "That Old Rockin' Chair's Got Me."

Wasn't that a wonderful meeting at the White House between Eisenhower and Kennedy? Eisenhower said, "Congratulations on your victory," and Kennedy replied, "I had to win. It's so tough these days to find a place that'll take children."

Have you heard about President Kennedy's new youth Peace Corps to help foreign countries? It's sort of Exodus with fraternity pins....and that Kennedy's press conferences were being beamed to Russia?...The Russians love the show—they've added a laugh track.

And what about Kennedy asking for two and a half billion more for his budget? He hasn't thrown out Ike's old budget—he's using it for petty cash. We expected some breakage in the White House, but that Caroline is too much.

Like Eisenhower, Kennedy was into golf, too. But he had more of a sense of humor about it. I remember once he and I played at the Seminole Country Club in Palm Beach with a great golfer and friend of Kennedy's, Chris Dunphy.

What a cast at this 1960 D.C. dinner honoring Eleanor Roosevelt. On the dais were Vice President-elect Lyndon Johnson and President-elect John Kennedy. In between introductions I waited on tables. And, let me tell you, for an audience full of politicians, the tips weren't half bad.

When the president turned up 20 minutes late on the first tee, Dunphy needled him about it. "I've been working on important things," Kennedy said.

They bet 10 dollars a hole. On the first green the president had a three-foot putt, a real little tester. "You're going to give me this putt, aren't you, Chris?" he inquired casually.

"It will develop your character," Dunphy said, deadpan.

"You mean to tell me I fly all the way down here to play with you and you won't give me a putt that long?"

"That's right," Dunphy replied. "If you make this, it's going to give you confidence."

1962. With President Kennedy and Dolores, wondering if I should have the gold medal assayed or bronzed.

Kennedy started to line up his putt. "I've got an appointment with Mortimer Kaplan, the head of the IRS, at 5:30," he said, eyeing Dunphy ominously. "So we'd better finish this game in a hurry."

"Pick it up," Chris said.

Of all the presidents, I would have to say that JFK had the nicest touch. He could have been a comedian himself. He also laughed harder than anybody (except perhaps LBJ, or maybe Roosevelt) at my jokes. There was the time he showed up at an Army-Navy football game in freezing weather without a hat or coat. "Things are tough, Mr. President," I told him, "but I'm sure we can afford to buy you a hat and coat. I'll even contribute a little myself." Two days later, by phone, he was still chuckling.

I first met Kennedy in 1958 when we both received

honorary degrees from Quincy University in Illinois. In September 1962 he presented me with the Congressional Gold Medal in the Rose Garden of the White House. I thanked him for the honor and said:

> *Mr. President, I feel very humble but I think I have the strength of character to fight it. There is one sobering thought—I received this medal for going out of the country. I think they're trying to tell me something.*

Inside the White House following the ceremony, I reminded Kennedy that the first time I saw him was at Quincy University. His response nearly brought tears to my eyes.

"The first time I saw *you* was on Wendy Island [in the South Pacific] during World War II when you gave a performance for those of us in the Navy there. Thank you for the laughs."

There were some major problems for the Kennedy "New Frontier" program that became a challenge for comedy. First was the Bay of Pigs—a plan designed by the CIA to eliminate the Cuban crisis. (It was the biggest fiasco since my first screen test.) Then there was Vietnam, trouble in Laos and a slight recession, and we were lagging in the space race, but laughter prevailed:

(TV monologue, May 13, 1961)

> *It's been a very depressing month. We're still behind in the space race, there's trouble in China, Laos and Vietnam. Right about now, Mr. Nixon must get the feeling he won. Things are so bad that last week Huntley tried to jump off Brinkley. Really, I don't envy President Kennedy. For the first time I'm worried if he has enough hair to last out the job.*

(In a personal appearance)

I made a telephone call from a pay phone the other day and when I put the dime in the slot, the AT&T operator said, "God bless you."

But, with the low points there was always a flip side. The Kennedy family and their activities always made good copy: Jacqueline wearing a short, albeit couturier, dress to church; JFK inviting cellist Pablo Casals to entertain "at home," playing touch football on the White House lawn, or taking 50-mile hikes; and brother Teddy running for senator of Massachusetts.

Imagine, a Kennedy willing to start at the bottom.

The monologues on my 1962 Christmas trip to the Far East echoed the same:

It's been a slow year back home—only one Kennedy got elected....The Kennedys had a nice Christmas: Jackie got a new pair of water skis, the president got a pair of hair clippers and Ted got a nice present—Massachusetts. There was a wonderful Christmas spirit in Washington this year. The Kennedys held a drive to raise money to buy toys for needy Republicans.

During my life I've had many trips to Washington, D.C. (I like to go to visit my money.) I was so honored when, from time to time, I would get a call from Pierre Salinger, Kennedy's press secretary, saying, "The boss would like to see you." They were casual visits where Kennedy just wanted to sit around and exchange jokes. On one of the visits, Kennedy said to one of his assistants, Dave Powers, "Tell Bob my favorite joke." Powers told me this one:

Another nose contest. This time at the request of President Kennedy with Robert S. Suggs Jr. of the White House police. I won by a freckle.

An Irishman died. His widow walked around the coffin and said, "He looks so good. And his toupee is on so straight. How did they do that?" And someone answered, "With a nail."

When I heard that was Kennedy's favorite, I offered him the use of my writers.

In November 1963 a thousand golden days of "Camelot" ended its run, to be replaced by "Dallas."

All the Kennedy jokes are still tinged with sadness. But I'll never forget that dynamic man who had the quickest wit of all the presidents. Laughter was a major part of the Kennedy persona and that is the image that prevails.

My big entrance into the White House Rose Garden. Emcee for the event was President Kennedy and the onlookers are my children: Tony, Kelly, Nora and Linda.

News and Short Takes from Camelot

First Lady Jacqueline Kennedy gives a TV tour of the White House:

I don't blame her for going on television. Look what it did for her husband.

Did you see all those beautiful oil paintings on the walls? George Washington crossing the Delaware with Bobby Kennedy standing beside him...And I didn't know Peter Lawford signed the Declaration of Independence.

No, Mrs. Kennedy said they were looking for paintings of authentic American history, like Crosby with his first son...Uncle Miltie [Berle] in a Paris gown...Zsa Zsa Gabor joining the PTA.

President Kennedy says we should all drink milk:

Maybe he's younger than we think. Milk—is he really Irish?

The Kennedy family is like the Strategic Air Command. They have somebody in the air at all times:

You all heard that President Kennedy will be visiting Palm Springs next week. He had to come—it's the only place a member of his family hasn't visited this month. He's visiting all the underdeveloped areas. Some of the houses there still don't have their own golf courses.

The president is flying to California, his wife is shopping in Italy and India and Bobby is traveling to Japan. Remember the good ol' days when you knew where the president was? On the golf course.

(TV monologue, September 27, 1963)
President Kennedy is just winding up a nonpolitical tour of the 11 states he lost in the last election. He wanted to see how they're getting along without federal aid.

A first-class first lady:

The president's wife just returned from a shopping trip around the world. It wasn't too successful. She couldn't decide which country to buy.

Isn't she beautiful? She's a wonderful answer to all this talk about the ugly American. I think we should put her in the State Department. She visited two countries and didn't have to duck once.

Her trip was sponsored by the International Association of World Peace, the International Committee for Refugee Child Welfare, and **Vogue** *magazine.*

JFK takes on U.S. Steel for price gouging:

(TV monologue, April 25, 1962)

The baseball season opened this month. In Washington President Kennedy threw out the first ball. He threw it at the president of U.S. Steel.

The White House press conference proved that the prez really has got a temper. The cherry trees blossomed three weeks earlier this year. I hate to think what'll happen if the price of haircuts ever goes up.

Kennedy was so mad he called the Cabinet, the Joint Chiefs of Staff, all his brothers and had the Atlantic Fleet anchor off Pittsburgh.

And I don't think it helped when the president of U.S. Steel, Roger Blough, visited the White House wearing his "I Like Ike" button.

And I wanna tell you one thing: They better not push Kennedy too hard. One of these days, he might give up the presidency and go back into money.

The race for space:

(TV monologue, November 29, 1962)

You know, when the Russian cosmonauts landed, Khrushchev kissed them. When our astronauts land, President Kennedy only shakes their hands. We may be behind in the space race, but at least we know what we're whistling at.

(TV monologue, September 27, 1963)

I guess you heard. The president suggested we join with the Russians to go to the moon. And Khrushchev was delighted. He said, "Today the moon, tomorrow Disneyland."

The Kennedy fitness program:

(TV monologue, March 13, 1963)

I just got back from Washington. I flew back. It was a little too far to walk. That walking bit is part of President Kennedy's physical fitness program. He's trying to get the country back on its feet.

…What a family. When they're not running for something, they're walking.

...The next flag may have 50 stars and a bunion.

...Bobby Kennedy is really in good shape; he went 50 miles. Imagine what he would do with [union leader] Jimmy Hoffa off his back.

...I guess the president wasn't kidding when he said we must proceed with "viga."

LYNDON BAINES JOHNSON

*When Charles de Gaulle got upset about the
devaluation of the British pound, he wired
Lyndon, "Lower your dollar." Johnson
wired back, "Up your francs."*

IT TOOK A LONG WHILE for the country to get
over the tragedy of Jack Kennedy's assassination but,
finally, Lyndon Baines Johnson was back in the saddle
and political business continued as usual. It became open
season again for anyone unfortunate enough to be getting free rent in the White House.

> *President Johnson says he wants to get started on his
> "Great Society." I don't know exactly how it's gonna
> work, but I think he wants Texas to adopt the rest of
> us…."Great Society"—it's the New Deal, with spurs.*

Yeah, like we understood every word he was saying.

As a senator from Texas, Democratic party leader and vice president under Kennedy, Lyndon Johnson had a tremendous influence. So as president of the United States he was bigger than life. His progressive legislation in civil rights, anti-poverty causes and Medicare, coupled with the downside of his administration—the escalation of the Vietnam War—were well documented by the press and the media.

And with all the attention, political humorists had a field day. Johnson wasn't much of a joke teller and of all the presidents I've known, he was the most sensitive to ridicule. It was well known that his nemesis was the dean (then and now) of press humorists, Art Buchwald. LBJ was not a happy camper when he found one of his staff laughing at what Art Buchwald had to say in his daily column.

And, like Truman, he became truly upset when First Lady "Lady Bird" Johnson and daughters Luci Baines and Lynda Bird were the subject of humorists.

Somehow, someway, LBJ did not think of me as a threat and what's more, I thought he was a great audience—

especially when the jokes were on him. I have a signed photo on my wall of LBJ, who is pictured almost under the table, laughing at this one:

One of the things that LBJ likes to do is to drive at unholy speeds across the state of Texas. Well, he was doing about 95 when this cop pulls him over and, without looking, starts to write him a ticket. As LBJ cranked down the window, the stricken officer realized his mistake:

"Oh, my God," he moaned.

"You'd better believe it," snapped the president.

Me and my straight man, LBJ, at the Washington Press Club dinner.

When the 1964 Democratic National Convention opened it was dominated by President Johnson and his slogan, "All the way with LBJ," which prompted:

Delegates to the Democratic convention didn't have tickets. To get in they had to show the LBJ brand, and it wasn't easy—when it wasn't on your arm.

The convention nominated LBJ and Hubert Humphrey as his running mate on the first ballot. It had all the suspense of a Russian election.

That year, LBJ asked me for some joke material for his presidential campaign against Senator Barry Goldwater. I got with the writers and sent him a few pages. In his letter of thanks, dated May 25, 1964, he took a stab at humor as he concluded, "I always suspected that you could do my job, but after seeing the quality of jokes that you must constantly produce, I know that I can never do yours." He may have thanked me for the jokes, but I'll be damned if I ever heard him use any.

But he was in top form that year when I was in D.C. to receive the USO Silver Medal. The prez himself was going to present the medal. The day before the dinner we were informed that pressing State matters had forced the president to cancel his appearance. So it was a pleasant shock when word rippled along the head table that the Johnson motorcade had pulled up to the side door of the Washington Hilton. As they were playing "Hail to the Chief" I was busy trying to decide which jokes I should now omit from my material.

When toastmaster John Daly said, "Ladies and gentlemen, the president of the United States," Johnson paused while the ballroom full of Cabinet members, congressmen, judges, military brass, industry executives, actors, agents and the media stood and applauded him. When the noise settled down he put on his glasses and said:

For grown-ups this beats the Easter egg roll on the White House lawn. Jerry Colonna delivered the joke. The rest of us—Johnny Grant, LBJ and my son Tony—enjoyed the laugh.

Mr. Chairman...Mr. Hope...ladies and gentlemen... I have come here today to honor a man with two very unusual traits. He is an actor, who is not, as far as I know, running for public office.

The audience loved his allusion to Ronald Reagan, and he continued:

*And he is a frequent visitor to Vietnam who has
never been asked to testify before the Senate Foreign
Relations Committee—at least, not yet.*

Obviously, the Senate was holding an investigation of
the nation's involvement in Vietnam.

*...I understand Bob was planning to testify until he
discovered there was live coverage on only one network, and it wasn't a friendly network. It isn't that
he wanted the additional exposure. It was just that
he refused to go up against the "I Love Lucy" rating
without some help.*

The audience was responding to him like he was one
of the nation's top comics.

*...It may come as a surprise to some people with
short memories that Bob Hope is more than a comedian. The book about his travels to entertain the
troops during World War II was called* **I Never Left
Home.** *Since then he has spent so much time with
our troops overseas that there are those who now say
he ought to write a sequel,* **I Never Came Back.**

He handed me the Silver Medal and sat down to my
left. He was a tough act to follow, but I tried:

*Thank you very much, Mr. President. [To the audi-
ence] Wasn't that a crazy drop-in? An extra chair
turned up fast, didn't it?*

*...It's nice to be back here in Washington. Or, as the
Republicans call it, Camp Runamuck....No, but it's
nice to be back here in Birdland.*

Johnson stared up at me. I stared back trying to read his face. In a lower voice I apologized:

I want you to know that this material was written without the knowledge that you were going to be here. I have to do it, it's here on the paper.

Both Johnson and the audience laughed. From that moment on, Johnson seemed to relish the straight-man role. He stared at me, then out at the audience, milking the applause and the laughter.

The last time I saw LBJ was down in Acapulco. He was enjoying his retirement. Dolores and I had taken our children and their spouses and our grandchildren to Tres Vegas for a week of golf and fishing. The prez was staying with his family at a private home nearby. Lynda Bird joined us for a day of deep-sea fishing and Dolores and I spent a delightful evening with Lady Bird and Lyndon.

LBJ's Comings and Goings

Johnson's proposed national budget, $196 billion:

It was a typical Texan's budget. It balances perfectly providing they strike oil under the White House.

Of course, no one knows what the president has in the back of his mind. He may be thinking of selling something—like Michigan.

One item in the budget is $50 million to fight crime. There's only one way to wipe out crime in this country: Put a tax on it. If it's high enough, nobody could afford to steal.

President Johnson was either consulting with me on a foreign policy problem or asking me the answer to 39-Down: an 8-letter word for "pain in the neck" beginning with "C" ending in "gress."

The "Great Society" program:

When we get the "great society," there'll be no more pain, no tension, no headaches, no stomach acid and no tired blood. It may be good for the country but it's gonna take all the fun out of commercials.

No one's figured out where we're going to get the money for all this. Maybe he's gonna put the entire country on the Diners Club card.

Yessir, the prez says he's gonna increase federal benefits, lower taxes, have Medicare for pets and we're all gonna be rich—I just wonder under which shell he hid the pea.

Johnson declares War on Poverty —"Lights out":

When the prez found out the electric light bill at the White House was running three thousand dollars a month, he turned out all the lights. Now, it's running three thousand a month for broken legs.

I was invited to stay at the White House but I didn't have a flashlight with me.

Lynda Bird just signed with **McCall's** *magazine as a writer and youth consultant. And you thought the president was kidding about his War on Poverty.*

I think Lynda Bird deserves a lot of credit for working. She could have gone into politics.

A "sleep-over" at the White House:

The president was very nice. It makes you feel good to have the president as your personal guide—you don't have to tip.

Like a true Texan, LBJ's got stereo everywhere, but it can be embarrassing. How'd you like to be washing your hands when the speaker blasts out "The Eyes of Texas Are Upon You?"

I got so shook up, I put back three towels. And one of 'em was from the Sheraton Hotel.

I guess all the talk about economizing is true. I wanted to wash my hands, but I didn't have a coin for the slot.

Reported feud with Bobby Kennedy:

Actually, the president and Bobby Kennedy are very good friends. They lunched together only yesterday. LBJ picked up the check…and Bobby paid the food taster.

Can you imagine a Texan having a conversation with a New Englander? I wonder who the interpreter was.

They really can't agree on anything. You know how LBJ turns out all the lights in the White House? Guess who sneaks around and turns them back on?

Bobby phoned LBJ in Texas and said he wasn't the least bit interested in the White House. What LBJ didn't like about it, Bobby was speaking from the Oval Office at the time.

Swimming in the White House pool:

If the president really likes you, he invites you to swim in the White House pool. And if you're a Democrat, he puts water in it.

You can tell the "in" group in Washington—they're all wet.

How about President Johnson's nude swimming? I just can't wait for the next TV tour of the White House.

...Isn't anything top secret anymore?

Last week LBJ held a Cabinet meeting in the pool and it worked very well. They talked to each other man to man.

On the road with LBJ:

(Asia, 1961)

Vice President Johnson is back from Asia. He had a little trouble with Pakistan. He can't understand people who aren't drilling for anything.

(Palm Springs, 1964)

President Johnson was in Palm Springs this weekend. I say if you're gonna fight poverty, go to the source.

I kept wondering if he gripped my hand any tighter, would it be against protocol to swat a president with a rolled-up speech.

(Asia, 1966)

The president is making a six-nation tour of Asia...
He is traveling throughout the Far East to make
friends. If it works, he may try it in this country.

...He's going to visit all our allies over there. He may be back the same day.

...There was one tense moment at the airport when leaving Washington. Vice President Humphrey held out his hand for the keys to the White House. LBJ finally handed them over but he said, "Remember, I've still got the Army, Navy and Texas."

The president's trip was a big success. He got six countries to accept foreign aid.

Johnson would like to make peace in Asia— he's running out of continents for Hubert Humphrey to tour.

(Hawaii, 1966)

How about President Johnson meeting with Vietnam's General Key in Hawaii? They've made a decision about Vietnam that should please everybody— they're going to close it down.

The prez is really an amazing man. What other guy would plan a trip to exotic, romantic Hawaii and take Dean Rusk [secretary of state] with him?

The president loves Hawaii. Nobody has the heart to tell him it's not part of Texas.

However, the president was pretty upset en route to Hawaii. The in-flight movie starred Ronald Reagan.

I'm holding on for dear life. With LBJ at the wheel, be it car or golf cart, the ride is a fast and frantic one. He played golf the same way. As I recall, I let him win....I didn't want to have my taxes audited.

(South America, 1967)

LBJ had a successful visit to South America. He got back.

...No, he loved South America. He thought it was part of Texas. Now it is.

...He really had a whirlwind tour. He was constantly on the move down there—that'll teach him not to drink the water.

(Guam, 1967)

Our president just got back from Guam. I didn't think we had voters there.

"Beautify, Beautify":

Remember Lady Bird's "Beautification of America" program? I know I'll never forget it. She called me up one day and suggested I hire a new makeup man.

She brought her Beautification Program to Los Angeles. She came to dedicate a national park. She left Old Faithful in Washington.

...Actually she flew over Los Angeles, took one look out the plane window and kept going. She's a typical Texan—she thought California was cute.

Lady Bird's TV tour of Washington:

The other night Lady Bird Johnson took us on a tour of Washington for one hour on television. That's as long as she could have it...then her husband took it back.

Actually, the tour was a public service program. It gave the Republicans a chance to see Washington, too.

The way the president and Mrs. Johnson describe Washington, you can tell they love it—sort of pride of ownership.

Lady Bird praised it so much that Lyndon is afraid that we might want it back.

And the First Lady's Beautification Program must be working—she didn't see one Republican.

Luci Baines Johnson weds Patrick Nugent:

It wasn't easy courting Luci. How'd you like to double date with two Secret Service men?

When Patrick popped the question, seven people said, "I do."

The president's happy. He figures he's not losing a daughter but gaining a voter.

The president is giving the bride away. He might as well, he's given everything else away.

Lynda Bird Johnson weds Charles Robb:

They're going to hold the wedding in Texas with over 2,000 guests. They're building a wing on the barbecue pit.

It's a typical Texas wedding. They're going to kiss the bride and brand the groom.

The wedding list is strictly nonpolitical. Some Republicans are invited—they need all the waiters they can get.

Yes, Luci is married and Lynda is married. Now, if only LBJ and Congress could find happiness.

The patter of little feet in the White House:

You've all heard—Luci and Patrick are expecting. Well, that's one thing you can't blame on the Republicans.

Just what the Democrats need—another mouth to feed.

LBJ's very happy about it. It's the first thing a Johnson has done that doesn't need approval from Congress.

They don't know if it's a boy or girl. The president hasn't decided yet.

They've already arranged for a baby-sitter. Well, there go Hubert Humphrey's weekends.

Gallbladder surgery:

I'm happy to report that the president is recovering nicely from his operation. Now we all know why he was so anxious for Medicare.

The operation was delayed for 48 hours while they found a surgeon who wasn't sore about Medicare.

It wasn't an easy operation for the surgeons. The president wouldn't let them turn the lights on.

President will not run:

The president's announcement that he wouldn't accept the nomination left the nation in shock. In fact, it was the first time Hubert Humphrey was speechless.

Have you noticed how popular Johnson's become since he said he wouldn't run again? That seems to be the trick. If there's anything Americans hate, it's to be rejected.

Lyndon and Lady Bird will be returning to Texas but nothing will change much. Having herds of cattle is a lot like politics—you have to watch your step.

RICHARD MILHOUS NIXON

I've had the pleasure of entertaining the presidents many times at dinners. I wasn't ordered. It had been more or less a suggestion from the IRS.

OF ALL THE PRESIDENTS I've known, I think Dick Nixon was perceived to be the least comfortable with humor. (Calvin Coolidge was before my time.) In public he seemed weighed down with worries. It appeared that jokes made him nervous and he seldom started a speech with one. But get him on a golf course and he was all smiles—at good jokes and some that weren't so good. So I had the pleasure of knowing a relaxed and smiling Vice President Nixon since 1953 when I referred to him as Ike's caddy. However...

Reflecting on his Quaker upbringing, Nixon, in his 1960 presidential campaign speeches, would, from time to time, include a caution to the youth of America and the

How's this as the national logo for "Ski America?"

leaders in government not to use profanity. Based on this truth, the story goes that:

> *After such a speech a prominent Republican from Jacksonville, Florida, approached Nixon and said, "Mr. Vice President, that was a damn fine speech." The vice president said, "I appreciate the compliment but not the language." The Republican went on. "I like it so much that I contributed a thousand dollars to your campaign." To which Nixon replied, "The hell you say."*

Nixon lost the 1960 race to John F. Kennedy. Many attributed the vice president's lack of humor as a major cause of his defeat. Nixon attributed his defeat to me. You see, my significant contribution to his 1960 campaign was to advise him to meet John Kennedy face-to-face in a televised debate. He reminded me of this fact every chance he got. And I always retorted that he lost the race for the governorship of California in 1962 all on his own. But, lest we forget, he was back on his feet for the 1968 presidential campaign and he was the only president who appeared on "Laugh-In."

There were many hopefuls in the race for the presidency in 1968:

I see that Vice President Humphrey has been transferred from Washington to the Far East. I guess the Democrats wanted him to get out of the combat area.

And I just heard that Bobby Kennedy has thrown his hair in the ring.

Georgia Governor Wallace was campaigning in Los Angeles. He took a tour around Watts—way around.

Governor Reagan's been on a nationwide tour, denying that he's a candidate. He's visited 49 of the 50 states so far, just to make it clear.

While Governor Rockefeller keeps insisting that he won't run, all I know is, he ordered towels with the presidential seal and his monogram on them.

...Senator Harold Stassen [Republican governor of Minnesota] just threw his hat in the ring for the seventh time. He had to run—32 years ago he got a great buy on buttons.

The Republicans are offering choices for the voters: They've got Reagan, who is a right-of-the-roader; Nixon, who's a left-of-the-roader; and Rockefeller, who owns the gas stations on it.

It's nice to have New York Mayor John Lindsay on the show. It's refreshing to meet a Republican who is not running for president.

After this I told Dinah Shore, "From now on, you stick to the singing, and I'll tell the jokes."

What a happy occasion when Richard Nixon asked Sammy Davis Jr., Les Brown and half of Hollywood to entertain at the Welcome Home dinner for Vietnam POWs in May 1973.

When the dust cleared, it was Nixon and Agnew vs. Humphrey and Muskie who provided the material for my TV monologues in the fall:

Humphrey and Nixon have both been vice president so they have one thing in common: They're both starved for affection.

Humphrey wants Nixon to debate him. Nixon refuses, and Hubert's having the same trouble with Nixon that he had in the White House—no one to talk to.... No, they keep asking Nixon why he won't debate Humphrey. That's like asking Rosemary why she won't have another baby. The Republicans are following Humphrey around with a "Truth Squad." And the Democrats have a "Truth Squad" following Nixon. Imagine that, truth in campaigning!

History recorded that Nixon won by a very narrow margin. How I covered it on my TV special the day after the election:

> *Well, it's over, and from force of habit Nixon has just conceded....Boy, what suspense! Alfred Hitchcock is demanding equal time. What a switch.*

> *What an election! Nixon was nervous. He kept saying, "Is it too late for a debate?" I could tell Nixon was nervous—he was giving the victory sign with one finger. It was the closest election in history. The lead changed hands faster than a fan dancer working in the round. But it was hardest on Spiro Agnew. Just when he was getting known, he becomes the vice president.*

Joke-telling was most certainly not Nixon's strong suit, even when the material belonged to somebody else. He used to tell the story about the two of us always being asked by photographers to look at each other so they could get a shot of the country's two most famous noses. He said that I quipped, "What a wonderful ad for Sun City." Actually, my line referred to our ski-slope noses and Sun Valley, Idaho. But, somehow, it was always funnier when he told it his way.

The political satirists followed every move of the Nixon presidency. So did I. My November and December 1968 monologues covered all the activities of president-elect Richard Nixon:

> *...Dick Nixon is traveling back and forth to Florida so much, we could have a surprise winter capital— Havana.*

...Did you hear that LBJ invited Dick and Pat Nixon to the White House? I think Nixon was a little anxious. He brought his luggage. The Johnsons brought out their best silver, no knives. The president showed the Nixons around the White House: the Lincoln bed, the Wilson library, the Harold Stassen wishing well.

...I saw Nixon in Palm Springs the other night at a Republican governors' dinner. I walked over to him and asked about his health and welfare and he said, "Sorry, that post is filled."

...And he just gave a top job to Professor Henry Kissinger of Harvard. He has to have someone in the government who understands [columnist] Bill Buckley.

In early 1969 President Nixon made a trip to Europe. To me and my writers it was a record-breaking tour for an American:

...He visited five foreign countries and didn't lend them a dime.

...He lunched with Queen Elizabeth at Buckingham Palace. They used the same solid gold plates that they used when I lunched at the palace, only this time they weren't chained to the table.

...He spent an afternoon in Paris with General Charles de Gaulle. Nixon told de Gaulle what a great man he was. And de Gaulle told Nixon what a great man de Gaulle was.

*...Spiro was very good handling the country while
Nixon was away. In fact, he didn't fall on his face
until Dick came back. No, he slipped at the airport
on some ice the Democrats left behind. Nixon looked
down and said, "What devotion!"*

I got some of the biggest laughs from Nixon when I
joked about his presidential residences, including the
log cabin in Whittier, California, he was building to be
born in.

*We have a White House in California. We have
a White House in Florida and the old place on
Pennsylvania Avenue—any day now, that could
become a Howard Johnsons. He's not going to stop
till he's got a branch in every state. Why should he
be different than Colonel Sanders?*

In December of 1969, while preparing for an overseas
Christmas tour to Vietnam to entertain our men and
women in uniform, I received a call from Nixon inviting
all the cast and crew to start the tour with rehearsals, a
show and dinner at the White House. The president said
what a great house it was to play in—once you break in
your act, you don't have to change it for four years.

The monologue went on:

*...Imagine, rehearsing in the White House.
That's like renting Carnegie Hall to crack your
knuckles....I think it was kind of the president
to extend the invitation to our troupe. I just wish it
hadn't started out, "Greetings."*

For years I have been looking for a format in which to

President Nixon just "dropped in" our backyard for a game of golf. That's some golf cart he brought along!

tell about the remarkable sensitivity expressed by Pat Nixon at this event. Prior to the Washington visit, the cast and crew were all schooled (or so I thought) in the protocol involved in attending a formal White House dinner. At the dinner the president sits on one side of the room and the first lady on the other. I was sitting with Pat Nixon and was horrified when I looked up and saw my traveling gypsies forming a line around the president's table asking for his autograph. Pat saw what was happening and, without a beat, reached for my place card, handed it to me and calmly said, "Bob, what a lovely tradition for us to start at the White House. May I have your autograph?" Funny? No! But what great timing. What a gracious hostess!

Dolores and I have been fortunate to have a few of the

We got a two-for-one-special on the coats. This was just prior to a golf game where he vowed he was going to get some of my vaudeville money.

presidents visit our home. But it was Nixon who made the grandest entrance of them all when he landed by helicopter in our backyard in Toluca Lake to play golf on January 3, 1970. He was expected but it caused quite a commotion in the neighborhood when four military helicopters circled the area and one landed 50 feet from the house. I went out to greet him, and as he stepped down he smiled and uncharacteristically quipped, "Is it all right if we park here?"

Six days later, at a dinner honoring another actor-turned-politician, Senator George Murphy, I had the opportunity to use the lawn arrival of Nixon with my turn at the podium:

I suppose you read where the president stopped by and changed his clothes at my house...which is now officially designated as the Richard Nixon Memorial Locker Room.

I guess the president is worrying about 1972. Why else would he be going house to house? But, that's the way it is with Republicans. Two weeks ago I had dinner at the White House, and Saturday I look up and there's the president on my doorstep.

Of course, it made me a big man on my block. From now on the sightseeing bus won't consider me just another rest stop.

He showed up at the Desert Classic a month later to play some golf with me. He actually chortled when he heard me tell of the outing:

I don't mean to call President Nixon a pigeon. That would be disrespectful. I won't even say who won the loot...but, if you look through the president's $200 billion budget, I'm in there somewhere!

There is one time that Nixon left me speechless in using him as joke material. It was November 1970. Dolores and I were in London for two command performances for royalty and to tape a talk show for Thames Television. Upon entering the Thames studio I was met by Eamonn Andrews, who said, "Bob Hope, This Is Your Life." Great, there I was in front of all of England without my writers—and just my ad-libs. My mind raced to my gag material on Nixon, who had recently visited London. Then, all of a sudden, on a big screen is the face of

President Richard Nixon, with serious glowing remarks about me. No laughs here. I had to wait until they showed a photograph of the house in Eltham where I was born to quip, "And we still owe some rent there."

In 1971 Nixon was on hand to dedicate the Eisenhower Medical Center in Palm Desert, California. It gave me the chance to comment about his pending visit to China in 1972:

He's been practicing eating with chopsticks. He hasn't got anything in his mouth yet, but he's started two fires.

Nixon is a real expert on China. He can order without a menu.

The tremendous success of the China trip and his sincerity to keep his promise of four years earlier to end the Vietnam War secured his chances of winning the Republican nomination in 1972 and a second term in the White House.

(TV monologue, March 1972)

Nixon's trip [to China] was an international success. A new poll shows that he has a better-than-ever chance of being re-elected president of this country, and a 40 percent chance of being elected president of China.

Some conservatives feared Mr. Nixon lost his shirt in China, but that's not true. Kissinger found the laundry ticket and he's going back for it.

The Russians blasted Nixon's trip to China.
They said the whole thing was to get Nixon re-elected.
I think that's kinda silly. How many Red Chinese
are registered Republicans?

Nixon won the 1972 election by a landslide, defeating
the Democratic ticket of George McGovern (senator of
South Dakota) and R. Sargent Shriver Jr. One of his first
acts was to change his Cabinet. Mr. Nixon asked everybody
to send in their resignation:

(TV monologue, February 1973)

The Nixon "V" sign we thought meant "victory."
To the Cabinet, it meant "vaya con Dios."

...It really upset Pat. She thought the job was steady.

...It's a strange sight at the unemployment office—
the Nixon Cabinet standing behind George
McGovern.

...Did you see the pictures in the papers of President
Nixon shopping in New York? I knew he was looking
for a new Cabinet...but in Hammacher-Schlemmer???

...But I think Dr. Kissinger will be staying on. It's
not easy to find a doctor who makes house calls all
over the world.

On January 28, 1973, Nixon's promise was kept. There
was a cease-fire in Vietnam. North Vietnam, it appeared,
finally qualified for foreign aid. Despite some remarkable
successes, all was not well in the Nixon camp. His admin-

istration started to unravel. The investigation of the 1972 Watergate break-in implicated Republican party officials, and Spiro Agnew resigned under pressure, pleading no contest to charges of income-tax evasion. House Minority Leader Gerald Ford replaced him as vice president.

A friend was in trouble and there was little to joke about and little to laugh at, but I tried.

...Watergate proved to the country how tough it is to find good plumbers today. Here I am on my first show of the season and I want to thank the Watergate Committee for making room for me.

...It appears that the president taped all his conversations in the Oval Office. I just hope that 18 minutes of missing tape included some of the bad jokes I told him.

...Presidents and vice presidents are leaving so fast that the White House is beginning to look like a Tijuana motel.

It's interesting that it was Nixon's press secretary Ron Ziegler who unintentionally put an ironic twist of humor on Nixon's problems.

Ziegler was recounting the accomplishments of the 1973 presidential year to a White House reporter, concluding that "it was an impressive year except for the downside." "What downside?" asked the reporter. "Watergate," said Ziegler.

Nixon resigned from office on August 9, 1974, and another vice president and golfer became the 38th president of the United States.

The great thing about commencement exercises is that you get to dress up and play Supreme Court judge. On this particular occasion, Richard Nixon and I received honorary doctorates from Whittier College (1965).

"Let Me Make This Perfectly Clear"

One of the problems that plagued President Nixon during his presidency in 1973 was inflation...

Unless the boys in Washington do something about inflation fast, the odds are two-to-one that five'll get you two.

The dollar's been stretched so far, George Washington now has a space between his teeth.

...and the energy crisis:

Mr. Nixon means business. Wait until Kissinger finds out he's coming back from Peking in a canoe.

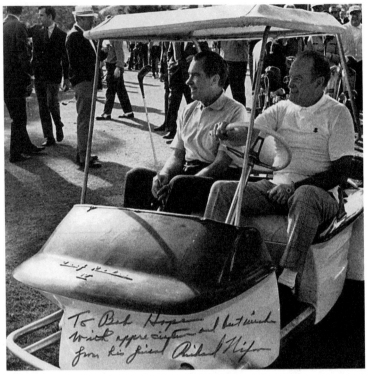

Golf with Richard Nixon at Lakeside Golf Club, Toluca Lake. Finally, a president who didn't want to be in the driver's seat.

To conserve heating fuel the president said we should keep our thermostats at 68. But the Democrats keep talking about '76.

When the president said to "slow down to 50," everybody took their foot off the accelerator. Now we have 10 million cases of self-inflicted whiplash.

And to conserve energy we're returning to daylight-saving time. Isn't that wonderful? Now that we can't do anything, Congress gives us an extra hour not to do it in.

Nixon was an avid football fan:

I know President Nixon is a big Redskins fan, but I think he's going too far when he uses the hot line to phone in a game plan to the bench.

I can understand why Nixon enjoys football and baseball so much. After Washington, it's such a nice change to see some teamwork.

Wedding bells for the Nixon daughters:

(Julie Nixon and Ike's grandson)

Now, whoever thought when Eisenhower and Nixon were running together, someday they'd get married? Isn't that nice, though...Julie Nixon marrying David Eisenhower. Maybe the Republicans have figured out a way to keep the White House permanently by homesteading.

(Tricia weds a Nader's Raider)

The Nixons are happy about the marriage of Tricia to Eddy Cox, even though he's a liberal.... Interesting, a Nixon marrying a liberal. We'll find out if those mixed marriages really work.

Imagine, another White House wedding! Well, it's cheaper than hiring a hall.

Tricia and Eddy are not going to live with Mom and Dad. They want a place that's a little more permanent.

Nixon visits with the Pope, 1970:

Even though Nixon never met a pope before, he made a lasting impression on Pope Paul. Right off the bat he asked how Mrs. Pope and the kids were.

Nixon loved the smile on the pope's face. It was calm and serene…the kind of a smile you often see on the face of a man who doesn't have to worry about being re-elected.

Presidential humor is always in, even when the president is out of office. Here's some Nixon humor in retrospect.

At the summer White House:

I'll never forget the first time Richard Nixon invited me to dinner at his San Clemente estate. When I got there he took me aside and said, "Remember, you serve from the left."

Kissinger:

Nixon's secretary of state was Henry Kissinger— the Dr. Ruth of diplomacy.

Watergate:

Nixon loved China. Over there they thought Watergate was a rice paddy.

I told Nixon to burn the tapes. He told me to burn my golf clubs.

GERALD RUDOLPH FORD

Some people remember presidents as Democrats or Republicans and others as being left wing or right wing. I remember them as having either a slice or a hook.

JERRY FORD HAS BECOME a good and close friend. Of all the presidents, he is the one I can call a pal. The fact that we share the same fascination with the game of golf and that he and Betty live near us in Palm Springs just may have something to do with it. He plays in my Desert Classic, and I wouldn't miss his annual tournament in Vail, Colorado.

Ford was and is such a wonderful subject for humor, no matter where he is—in the White House, at home, on the golf course or in the locker room. And he not only laughs at the jokes I tell at his expense but he can dish it out, too. To illustrate, he got even with me when I asked him to write the foreword to my golf book:

Writing a foreword may be the only way for me to get a word in edgewise. I'd like to think that being a former president is something special. Not with Hope. I'm just another target for his sandbagging bets on the golf course and his big laughs onstage.

We play golf together often. I win, he wins; I lose, he loses; I pay, he tells a joke! If I could have one special Hope memento given to me, it would be the first dollar Bob Hope ever paid on a bet lost on a golf course. The search for that bill wouldn't be difficult. It's still in Bob's right-hand pants pocket.

Having sat in the hot seat in the White House, I can tell you that the press corps in Washington can give you a pretty good "working over." The treatment they gave me was nothing compared to what Hope says about me.

Bob and I have a lot in common. We both obviously love the game, its challenge, camaraderie and beauty. And, we both have run out of excuses or explanations for Betty and Dolores as to why the lure of the links still is like a siren's call to both of us. In thinking why they put up with us, I remember a wonderful line from Hubert Humphrey, "Some women marry below themselves." Hubert was a friend and probably would have been able to handle Hope for me. Unfortunately, Hubert didn't play golf.

Jerry and his antics and accidents on the golf course have given me some of my best material. For starters:

What an endorsement for the Pepsodent generation. Jerry and Betty Ford with Dolores and me at our home in Palm Springs.

...There are 42 golf courses in the Palm Springs area and nobody knows which one Ford is playing until he hits his tee shot!

...It's not hard to find Jerry Ford on a golf course— you just follow the wounded.

...Jerry Ford has made golf a contact sport.

...Jerry Ford is a hit man for the PGA.

However, there is more to Jerry Ford than just his golf profile. It may not be as important, but he *was* the 38th president of the United States. Assuming the presidency following Nixon's resignation was not an easy task. The chair in the Oval Office was a hot seat. There were economic difficulties, and the Democrat-controlled Congress resisted his domestic and external initiatives and even gave him a bad time by delaying approval of his choice of Nelson Rockefeller for vice president. But I had a ball.

He was in office less than two months and already I had the opportunity to zero in on his presidency with my September 1974 monologue:

...Ford is very down-to-earth. He's been president nearly two months now, and he still swims in the White House pool. Not once has he tried to walk across it....He's a real American. And if he keeps up the good work, he could be in the next Coke commercial.

...I played golf with him a few times before he became president—when I still had a chance of winning.

...Congress is sure taking its time to confirm Rockefeller. If they don't move fast a lot of their credit cards will be canceled.

...I hope Rocky is confirmed. It's what we've always needed: a politician who pays more taxes than we do....And a lot of people are surprised at Ford picking Rocky because, after all, Rocky's been trying to get the job of president for 12 years. That's like asking Morris the cat to watch your tuna sandwich.

By the time my Christmas show came around that year, the good news was that Rockefeller had been confirmed as vice president; the bad news was that the nation was in a recession and Ford was asking everybody to tighten their belts and embrace his WIN (Whip Inflation Now) button campaign:

...They're getting ready for yuletide at the White House: This morning, two wise men appeared on the lawn. There used to be three, but you know how Ford's been cutting down.

...But it's thrilling to hear, in the middle of the recession, that someone got a job, especially such a deserving case as Nelson Rockefeller....Doesn't it give you a warm feeling to know we're living in a country where any multimillionaire can become vice president?

...With Rocky as vice president it takes a load off the president's shoulders. Now he doesn't have to worry about meeting the national debt. He just slips it under Rocky's phone bill and lets it go at that.

And Ford had just returned from an overseas trip to Japan, Korea and Russia—all Republican strongholds:

...The trip to Japan was quite successful. They were happy to meet the man who runs the country they own. Hirohito gave the president a jeweled sword with a crest of the Imperial Order of the Setting Sun, and the president gave him a WIN button. The president told him, "Millions of Americans are wearing these." And Hirohito said, "I know. We make them."

Either I was getting brash in assuming that there was always a spare room waiting for me, or the hospitality of Betty Ford always made me feel at home, but my stays at the Ford White House were more relaxed than visits with previous presidents.

Dolores and I loved being in the private quarters on the second floor where we kicked off our shoes, put our feet up and just talked and laughed.

According to Betty: "Bob loved staying there. In fact, he enjoyed it so much he once asked if he could be adopted. And he only tried sitting in the Oval Office once."

Many perceived Ford as an unusual choice for a president. Although he graduated from the University of Michigan and Yale Law School, was a Naval lieutenant commander stationed in the Pacific during World War II and served in Congress for 25 years (eight as Republican leader), the public thought of him as a likable, friendly football player. And, what's more, not a particularly well-coordinated football player.

It doesn't take much for the political wits to stampede an individual. And Ford gave them the opening early in the game. First, he fell down a ramp when he and Betty were disembarking from an airliner in Munich. Then, boarding a military helicopter, he banged his head on the door. All of these incidents were, of course, well recorded in photos and print and on video.

The die was cast and he was labeled, and wrongfully so, as clumsy. And his "clumsiness" was exaggerated to the fullest extent. Ford did not relish this image but he knew it came with the territory and took his lumps (bad choice of words) and rolled with the punches.

He was a good sport and laughed along with those who kidded him. At the Washington Press Club he said, "I don't agree with those who call me the Evel Knievel of politics." He even invited Chevy Chase, who was without mercy in his mockery of Ford on "Saturday Night Live," to the annual dinner of the Radio and Television Correspondents Association at the Washington Hilton on March 13, 1975. I emceed the event, and when I introduced President Ford he got up from the table,

(Above) This was club day. The next day they gave us golf balls to play with.

(Left) Showing Jerry a new putting stance on the green. He believed me; he tried it. What's most surprising, it has improved his game.

"accidentally" caught the tablecloth in his trousers and dumped silverware in Chase's lap. He continued on, and as he approached the podium, he pretended to trip, sending the pages of the speech he was carrying flying out into the audience. Dan Rather, Walter Cronkite and others rushed to retrieve them. The room exploded with laughter. When he got to the microphone and things quieted down, the president reached into his coat pocket, pulled out the real script and said, "Good evening. I'm Gerald Ford and you're not." Again, the room rocked with laughter. Some labeled this as "shtick." To me, it was inspired comedy. I only wish he had warned me in advance that he was breaking in a new act. But, then again, I wouldn't have enjoyed the surprise of his performance.

Ford was well aware that humor could be a great defusing mechanism. To lighten his critics' accusation of "feet dragging" in asking for the resignation of his secretary of agriculture Earl Butz for telling a particularly offensive joke, he used humor in his statement following my introduction of him at the National Entertainment Conference in D.C.

It made all the newspapers:

I have only one thing to say about a program that calls for me to follow Bob Hope—it's ridiculous. Bob Hope has stage presence, comedy timing and the finest writers in the business. I'm standing here in a rented tuxedo—with three jokes from Earl Butz.

Ford was the first president, that I know of, to hire a comedy writer for his staff. Bob Orben was his name. But, as good as he was, he couldn't always keep the prez from lousing up a punch line. For instance, when Ford addressed a group of college athletic directors he said, "I feel very much at home here today, because the athletic director of any college and the president of the United

States have a great deal in common. We both need the talent, we both need the cooperation of others and we both have a certain lack of performance in our jobs." The word he was reaching for, of course, was *permanence.*

For diplomacy's sake, and to rest up for the 1976 election battle, Jerry Ford, along with Betty and daughter Susan, paid a visit to China. According to my December 1975 monologue:

...Hey, the president had a fine time in Peking.
He took along his wife and daughter. He heard that
with three you get egg roll.

...He loved China, and why not? Eight hundred
million people and not one of them is Ronnie Reagan.

...And Susan Ford loved the Great Wall. She said
her father often spoke of the Great Wall, only he
called it "Congress."

...The big hit of the trip was when Betty Ford
joined a group of Chinese dancers. She was so good
and everyone was impressed. Now we know where
our tax dollars have been going—dance lessons at
Arthur Murray's.

I think it's a mistake for Ford to underestimate
Reagan. Remember, for years he was at Warner
Brothers, and never lost a war.

Ford captured the Republican nomination away from Ronald Reagan. It wasn't easy—that actor was gaining momentum. His Democratic opponent was a peanut farmer–turned–governor of Georgia.

During the campaign the two candidates stayed at many of the same hotels. On one broadcast I said:

Of course, Ford tried to get there first. That meant more impact, more voters and less peanut shells in the beds.

On the campaign trail Ford kidded himself about everything. He created, in a sense, "Fordisms." To a convention of skiers he said, "I can ski for hours on end." About his golf he joked, "Arnold Palmer has asked me not to wear his slacks except under an assumed name." At Ohio State he quipped, "I met Woody Hayes at the airport. We had our picture taken...and the caption read 'Woody Hayes and Friend." At one outing he offered, "If Lincoln were alive today, he'd roll over in his grave."

You don't need a history lesson to know that Ford was edged out of the presidency by that peanut farmer.

But it was not President Jerry Ford I got to know and like so well. It is "former President" Ford who has become such a good friend.

It is Ford the golfer and Ford the joke maker and his wife, Betty, who Dolores and I enjoy spending time with. May he always be remembered for his most famous quote: "Fore."

These Are the Jokes, Folks!

At home with the Fords:

The whole Ford family, Betty and the children, Susan, Jack, Mike and Steve, are out campaigning for Jerry. They're so all-American, every time I see them together I get the feeling they're going to do an orange juice commercial.

How about Betty Ford calling people in New Hampshire hoping to get their vote? It's kind of like Dial-a-Prayer in reverse.

...So that's why they asked me to pay my taxes in dimes.

...They used to try to get the uncommitted vote. Now they try to get the unlisted.

It's been said that "behind every great man is a woman."...For Betty Ford, that's a double blessing. The way Jerry plays golf, that's the safest place to be.

The only thing I remember about this photo with Jerry Ford is that we were up to no good. Anyway, one of us won an award.

Did you read where the president's son, Jack, is dating tennis star Chris Evert? It must be odd for Jack to go out with a girl who's younger than he is and makes more money than his father.

Betty Ford is very pleased with her children. She doesn't care what they do...as long as they don't discuss it on the 6 o'clock news.

The Jerry Fords move to Palm Springs:

All of us in Palm Springs are thrilled that the Fords moved there. And Betty is the envy of every housewife in the area. Who else could tell an ex-president to take out the garbage?

Betty is known as our first lady of the desert. And Jerry is known as the last man out of the sand trap.

What else already—some more golf one-liners:

Ford was the first president to use a lethal weapon...a golf club.

His wife founded the Betty Ford Center, which can cure anything except Jerry's slice.

I love playing golf with Gerald Ford. He makes me feel like I'm back performing in a war zone.

Actually, we get along well on the golf course. I never remind him that he used to be the president and he never reminds me that I used to be funny.

Attorney Gerald R. Ford:

Jerry Ford used to be a lawyer....He went into politics when the judge wouldn't let him wear his skis in court.

Three of his clients are still on death row for parking tickets.

Ford takes on the CIA:

William Colby, head of the CIA, is out. The president wants to fire some more CIA men, but he doesn't know who they are.

Just what do ex-presidents do?

Jerry Ford may have trouble finding a suitable job. How many jobs do you see in the classifieds specifying "Must be ex-president"?

*Now, after 30 years of government, he has to go out
and try to find honest work.*

*...He turned down a couple of job offers. One was
to usher at a Ronald Reagan film festival.*

*He'd like a job where he doesn't have to do
anything or doesn't have to work every day—but he
doesn't want to return to Congress.*

*How about President Ford getting a job with NBC?
They're always hiring ex-football players.*

Ford's farewell State of the Union speech deserved
comment:

(Personal appearance, January 1977)

*Did you hear President Ford's farewell speech?
He said, "This will be my last State of the Union
address—maybe." The Republicans cheered,
the Democrats laughed and Ronnie Reagan put his
foot through the TV set.*

*...I don't know what that meant. Maybe he's going
to arm wrestle Jimmy Carter for the Oval Office.*

*But he's got to have something in mind. He hasn't
opened any of his going-away gifts.*

*"Goodbye...maybe." I've heard Zsa Zsa Gabor
more positive while taking her wedding vows.*

JAMES EARL CARTER

Mr. Carter spent 30 years growing peanuts, and now he's got a whole Congress that sticks to the roof of his mouth.

FINDING MATERIAL ON James Earl (Jimmy) Carter was probably the easiest chore my writers ever had. Here is a churchgoing peanut farmer from Plains, Georgia, who had a brother who brewed his own beer, an outspoken mother named Miss Lillian and a Southern accent so heavy that two mock dictionaries were published to help people understand him (i.e., har: a growth covering the skull). All these elements plus an infectious smile and a great sense of humor worked to his advantage.

This warm, unassuming gentleman, who seemed to come from nowhere, emerged as the winner of the Democratic primaries in 1976. When he accepted the nomination at the Democratic convention he smiled and said: "My name is Jimmy Carter and I'm running for president." On the campaign trail he talked about his liabilities: "I'm not from Washington, I'm not a member of Congress and I have never been part of the national government." He also said, "I will never lie to you."

You think he was smiling and inviting me in to the White House? What he was actually saying was, "I dare you to cross this line." But seriously, Jimmy Carter was such a gracious host that I returned the towels I'd taken when a Republican president was in residence.

Campaign manager Jody Powell commented, "We're going to lose the liar vote." And Jimmy's mother, Miss Lillian, countered with, "Well, I lie all the time. I have to—to balance the family ticket."

Well, Carter won his way into the hearts of the American public and won the presidency over the incumbent, Jerry Ford.

Everybody had fun with the Jimmy Carter/Walter

Mondale inauguration. The event dominated my January 1977 monologue:

It's official. Jimmy Carter has changed his address from Plains, Georgia, to "Down the road a piece."

...Did you see the size of that crowd at the Inaugural Parade? Jimmy said, "Y'all come," and they did.

...The swearing-in ceremony was out in the open. The Democrats applauded Jimmy Carter. The Republicans applauded the pigeons.

...The Inaugural Ball had a Southern flavor. It was the first time "Hail to the Chief" was played on a jug and washboard.

The humorists, the cartoonists and the media...everybody enjoyed the relaxed Southern-style White House. And me? You betcha! How about my March 1977 TV monologue:

...Spring came to Washington, D.C. It's official: President Carter took off his sweater.

...Mr. Carter is the first president we've had who considers a three-piece suit a sweater and two elbow patches.

And the president took his easy Southern way to the airwaves with a radio talk show where the public could have a one-on-one chat with their president. The way the show worked—you called in and the president phoned you back. I asked my TV audience:

Did you hear President Carter's talk show? Sounded like a two-hour commercial for Southern Comfort.

...He got calls from people who never get to talk to the president—like kids, the poor and the vice president.

...Two callers asked Carter about taxes and he admitted he didn't know the answers. How about that? Do we really need a president who's just like the rest of us? I mean, wasn't it nice that he didn't know anything? Instead of proving it?

...Teddy Roosevelt asked us to "walk softly and carry a big stick." And it was John Kennedy who said, "Ask not what your country can do for you, but what you can do for your country." Now we have a president who says, "Y'all call collect, y'hear?"

President Jimmy Carter let me borrow his podium and logo at a White House reception. The quartet ready to go on after my opening: USO President Chapman Cox, Dolores, First Lady Rosalynn Carter and the Prez.

My back-up duo for this White House gig was none other than President Jimmy and First Lady Rosalynn Carter.

...The talk show was so successful, Carter's decided to become the first president ever to be listed in the Yellow Pages.

...Billy Carter tried to call in, but it's pretty hard to reach the White House from Plains, Georgia, just talking through a beer can and a string.

Ah, Billy Carter. He was wonderful copy no matter where he went or what he did. He was outspoken, established his own labeled beverage, Billy Beer, and at one time, much to the shock of his brother, dabbled in foreign relations. To a man of less stature than President Jimmy Carter, this might have been a major disadvantage. But Jimmy Carter openly embraced Billy with love, compassion and yes, a sense of humor...as did the nation.

You can imagine how surprised and touched I was when I learned of the involvement of Jimmy Carter and his family, in my 75th birthday celebration. There was to be an NBC television special from the Kennedy Center in Washington, a tribute by Congress, lunch with House Speaker Tip O'Neill and a USO party—all topped off with a reception at the White House.

The two-day affair started off with a luncheon honoring First Lady Rosalynn Carter, hosted by the people who really control Washington, the congressional wives. Following the luncheon, we went to the White House for a 5 p.m. reception in the East Room, where 500 guests—dignitaries, the stars and production staff of the television special—had gathered. President and Mrs. Carter and daughter Amy greeted us. The president asked us to stand by his side and he took over as "top banana." He said:

I want to congratulate Bob Hope. He's getting ready to start a second career. He'll be making commercials full-time—advertising yogurt. Since Mr. Hope has now been proven to be 75 years old, at least we know his claim is false that he sold Pepsodent to George Washington. We all know that he had wooden teeth and he was a Lemon Pledge man. I'm talking about George Washington.

I've been in office 489 days.…In three more weeks I'll have stayed overnight in the White House as many times as Bob Hope has.

I'll never forget when we first moved in. We went by the Lincoln Room, and Rosalynn was really excited. We came here to the East Room and saw the portrait of George Washington and his first lady; I was excited. And Amy was excited in all the other rooms, because they had signs above the doors, Bob Hope Slept Here.

Amy is out there somewhere.

...I think I was the only person in the Armed Forces who'd never met him while I was overseas. Every Christmas Eve we would put some cookies and a bottle of scotch under our periscope in the submarine, but he never showed up.

Hey, this man was too funny. I wanted him to stay president just to keep him away from the comedy clubs.

I didn't need the competition. I cautioned him about being too funny and said:

I've never seen so many freeloaders in my life....
What a kick to shake hands with the president and
first lady....Thank you, President and Mrs. Carter, for
lending us your house....God knows, we paid for it.

The next day, I got one of the thrills of my life when I was recognized from the floor of Congress. All of the members got together and, for the first time in harmony, sang:

Thanks for the memories
Of golf with Tip and Ford
None of us ignored,
It sure took guts to sink those putts
Which showed how well you scored,
How lovely it was.
With the Republicans at the White House
you've feasted.
With the Democrats at the White House
you've fasted.
Oh, it was swell while it lasted.
Now Carter's here
Serving Billy Beer...

The country had nothing but praise and hope for the 1978 Camp David accord on peace in the Middle East, which was brokered by the president. For a change, my jokes were of a positive nature.

...Jimmy did so well at Camp David that now he's
thinking about sending Congress to camp.

...When the polls came out showing Carter's popularity had risen 11 percent, everyone went wild in the White House. They say Gatorade flowed like water.

In September of 1980, Dolores and I, together with friends the Clark Cliffords, the Stuart Symingtons and the Alex Spanoses, took off on the road to Moscow, Scotland and England. I had been asked to entertain the American community in Moscow. Being an election year, the Carter-Reagan jokes were the crowd favorites:

...Jimmy Carter is hoping Billy is born again, and he comes back as Ronald Reagan's brother.

...I was hoping Reagan would pick Charlton Heston for his vice presidential running mate— we need a miracle.

Things were not going too well for President Carter. There was a recession, inflation and unemployment were up and the dollar was down. Carter said the problems could be solved, and I was waiting for the announcement of his trip to Lourdes. The one time humor played no part was during the Iranian hostage situation, which did not get resolved until after President Carter left office. And he left office as he entered it, a gentleman with a "bodacious" smile.

I had a lot of fun with Jimmy Carter, even though he wasn't much of a golfer. After his term was up he continued his work as a peacemaker and a man dedicated to helping the poor. President and Mrs. Carter asked me to join them in support of their favorite charity, Habitat for Humanity. The Carters actually build houses for the poor. So I donned my hardhat and grabbed a hammer.

I helped Jimmy Carter build a house for Habitat for Humanity. Of course, he had to show me which end of the nail to pound. It didn't bother him, though—he had to work with Congress for four years.

The prez and I traded quips and raised awareness for a great cause.

Put Your Hands Together for Jimmy Carter

Presidential campaign, 1976:

(TV monologue, July 4, 1976):

Any country that can survive the hijinks in Washington, D.C., for 200 years deserves a salute.... Things really haven't changed in 200 years: George Washington didn't want to be president. He wanted to go home and be a gentleman farmer...Same with Thomas Jefferson. He wanted to go home and be a gentleman farmer. And now, 200 years later, Ford and Reagan and [Jerry] Brown want Carter to go home and be a gentleman farmer.

Look who's fighting it out for president—a farmer, a football player and an actor.

Brother Billy:

We have been blessed by great leaders who left us a legacy of wisdom. Like Franklin Roosevelt, who said, "We have nothing to fear but fear itself," and Harry Truman, who said, "The buck stops here"... and President Jimmy Carter, who said, "If Billy calls, tell him I'm out."

How about Billy Carter starting his own beer company? He did his brother one better. He found a way to spread gas without going into politics.

Amy growing up in the White House:

Rosalynn told reporters she was thrilled because Amy had just gone out on her first date—with a 15-year-old nuclear physicist.

Even with all those Secret Service men along, their date was very romantic. They walked arm-in-arm-in-arm...

Entertaining at the White House, Southern style:

They have new chinaware for the White House dining room. Rosalynn Carter says, however, that she was satisfied with the old White House china pattern—grits go with anything.

This is called a presidential standoff: You show me your smile and I'll show you mine.

Somehow she failed to mention all the china Jimmy had to replace following every dinner party brother Billy attended.

I hear one White House staff member has already broken one of the new plates. If you care to send condolences, he can be reached in care of our embassy in Libya.

Jimmy Carter has a great smile; a great dentist!

...Every time he grins, someone tries to write "Steinway" on his upper lip.

...The other day his teeth got up two hours before he did.

Jimmy is very Southern and very religious:

When he prays, he calls God by his first name— "Y'all."

And with all the Southerners around now, we'll all be talking like the Carters. The national anthem is going to start off "Oh, say can y'all see."

Carter picks his Cabinet:

Carter is picking his new Cabinet. It's a combination of Early American and Georgia Pine.

Carter had a hard time picking his Cabinet. Two thousand jobs to fill and only 32 relatives.

For national security adviser he picked Zbigniew Brzezinski. Say it fast and you'll never have to buy a Water Pik.

And you know, Amy asked for a job. Jimmy had a hard time convincing her that we don't have an ambassador to Disneyland.

All the other presidents took trips, why not Jimmy Carter?

How about President Carter's overseas trips? He went to Poland, Iran, Syria, Belgium and India. And on the second day...No, we don't know why he went to five countries, unless the sale of peanut butter was way down.

*It was great to see each nation make him feel
at home, especially with the food. In Poland they
served him grits and kielbasa; in India they made
him curried grits; in France, grits a l'orange and
in Iran, grits in oil—30 weight.*

My favorite story and comments about Miss Lillian:

*On the plane back from Europe Miss Lillian
won a bundle playing poker. It's the first time any
American has gone overseas on a diplomatic
mission and come back with more money than
he or she left with.*

The peanut farmer:

*Carter wants to go to Washington. He'll feel right
at home there—he was raised on a nut farm.*

RONALD WILSON REAGAN

I love to see politicians pray. It keeps their hands out where you can see what they're doing.

REAGAN ELEVATED THE JOKE to an art form. And no one has used it better. In my opinion Ronald Reagan is undoubtedly the best communicator we've had in the White House. With all that experience, when he got on the tube he was a hard man to resist. And he was so damn honest I can't understand how he ever became a politician.

My joke file on Ronald Reagan is the thickest. I'm not sure if it's because I have more material on him or, as I get older, the type gets larger and there are fewer jokes per page. Anyway, although I bought a cup of coffee for Yale student Jerry Ford in the late '30s, it is Ronald Reagan I've actually known the longest...since he was fresh to Hollywood from a job as a sportscaster in Des Moines,

Iowa, or as a lifeguard in Dixon, Illinois. (I've used both stories.)

I used to see him at Leucocyte Golf Club a lot. He came to the club one day, looked at me expectantly and said, "Hey, Bob, notice anything different about me?" I looked him up and down, and he looked like he always looked. "You got me," I said. "Contact lenses," he said, popping his eyeballs.

Granted, not his best material but an indication of the direction he was going...as an actor, that is, not as a governor and certainly not as the president of the United States.

Performer or politician, being resourceful is a must. And early in the game, Ronald Reagan was resourceful. During World War II the War Department created the Armed Forces Radio Services (AFRS) to broadcast to our troops. Every star in Hollywood contributed his or her service from time to time. Several of my writers, on the other hand, escaped there, where as privates they were actually paid for their services. Albeit, only $20 a month, but they were paid, I constantly reminded them.

AFRS was headquartered in Hollywood on the corner of Western and Sunset. It was a military madhouse, and trying to impose any kind of Army discipline on comedy writers was a joke in itself. So the story goes:

For a while, an actor named Captain Ronald Reagan put in a short hitch at AFRS headquarters. Captain Reagan's only military experience up to that time had been saluting Colonel Jack Warner [Warner Bros.] whenever Ronnie's option came up. On one carefree occasion, someone decided to make Reagan officer of the day. One of my writers who was part of the unit phoned him, disguising his voice.

"Captain Reagan? This is Lieutenant Colonel Whitney of the 54th, on secret orders from General McNair. I have a company of 100 men en route to Camp Roberts and we're running late. Can you provide bivouac?"

There was a short pause while Ronnie consulted his military dictionary.

"Yes, sir!" he replied, and immediately hung up and called Abbey Rents to deliver a hundred army cots.

The telephone rang again.

"Lieutenant Colonel Whitney here. Very sorry, I miscounted, captain. Our unit on the maneuver actually consists of 150 men. Does that present any logistical problem?"

"The impossible we do immediately," Reagan said, believing he had just coined a phrase. He hung up and phoned Abbey Rents for 50 more cots.

Then came the final phone call.

"Captain Reagan? You know, of course, the 54th is a cavalry unit. Be sure you have enough hay." And the "colonel" hung up.

Ronnie phoned the prop department at Warner Bros. They tell me there was straw blowing around in the wind on Sunset and Western for weeks after that.

I don't know if the country is aware of it, but during his acting days Ronald Reagan was a bona fide Democrat. Then all of a sudden he got religion, or something, and was running for governor of California as a Republican:

(Test Pilot dinner, 1966)

Reagan claims that if he's elected he'll give up acting—what a sneaky way of getting votes....But it's now or never for Reagan. Let's face it, it may be a hundred years before that hairdo's in style again.

And he was elected already. At a WAIF benefit in Los Angeles in 1968 I had a chance to comment:

I don't do warm-ups for just anybody. But it's always nice to give a fellow actor a helping hand now and then.

*It's nice to see Governor and Mrs. Reagan here
tonight. But I was delighted when he went to
Sacramento. We used to compete for the same parts.
Then our paths separated. He went into politics
and I went straight.*

*The good thing about the election: It restored this
country to a two-party system—the Democrats and
the actors.*

During his "tour" as governor of California, his material, TV appearances and concerts reflected Reagan's presidential aspirations:

(1968)

*...Everybody's getting into the act. Humphrey's running...Rockefeller's running...and Ronald Reagan's
crouched at the starting gate. The Republicans
have a problem with Reagan. He won't run for the
presidency without script approval.*

(1969)

*...There's talk that Ronnie has his eye on the White
House—which is not easy now, since Nixon has
three of them.*

(1970)

*...Ronnie is running for governor of California
again, which crosses up the smart boys—they
thought he'd be satisfied with just the White House.*

(1971)

...Can you imagine what would happen if Reagan was elected president? Instead of postage stamps, we'd have eight-by-ten glossies.

(1972)

...The governor and Nancy are back from Washington, D.C. He took a tour of the hotel they were staying in. He wanted to see the presidential suite.

(1973)

...It's no secret that Reagan wants to move from Sacramento to Washington—which is like getting promoted to captain just before the iceberg hit the Titanic.

(1974)

...I have a hunch that Reagan is serious about the presidency. He called his makeup man and had his temples grayed and his wrinkles put back in.

Reagan got even with me. In 1975, just prior to exiting from the governorship of California to run in the Republican primaries for president, Reagan was in rare form on a televised Dean Martin roast—at my expense. His competition on the dais included Jack Benny, Milton Berle, General Omar Bradley, Howard Cosell, Reverend Billy Graham, Martin himself, Don Rickles, Nipsey Russell, Jimmy Stewart and Flip Wilson. Reagan approached the lectern, looked to his left at me and smiled; he looked to his right and thanked Dean Martin and then took aim and fired:

At a 1980 Reagan campaign rally in Peoria, Illinois. Only one of these guys didn't make president.

I was a little surprised when I was asked to be here tonight to honor Bob Hope. Well, "surprised" isn't exactly the right word—I was annoyed. I've got a lot of important decisions to make in the next several weeks, like, do I go with Bekins or stick with U-Haul?

Now, in accepting this invitation, I don't want the taxpayers to think that I'd make a special trip down here just to be on this program. Now, that would be frivolous. I just happened to be in town anyway, for something really important—a guest shot on "Hollywood Squares."

*Seriously, Bob would do well in politics. He
certainly has to be one of the most familiar faces in
America. He's entertained over 10 million troops;
been seen by more than 100 million TV viewers;
and, if you throw in the 27 people who've seen his
movies, you have a pretty sizable constituency.*

*Of course, I'm the last to criticize somebody's movie
career. I've had a few disasters myself. I don't
criticize governors, either.*

*Bob Hope is a man of remarkable accomplishment.
He's been America's favorite comedian at a time
when America was in her most bewildered state of
mind. He's entertained six presidents....he's
performed for 12.*

*Seriously, Bob, I know that over the years you've
received many tributes and awards and it gives me
great pleasure to tell you that in honor of this occasion,
the state legislature has unanimously passed a bill
naming you California's foremost citizen. I vetoed it.*

He outshone everyone on the dais, save one. Leave it
to my wife Dolores to top him. She approached the microphone and admonished everyone, saying, "All evening
I've sat here while you've made fun of and criticized my
husband. All I can say is, 'Hear! Hear!'"

With that quality of material and performance, Reagan
should have won the primaries in 1976, but he lost out to
the Ford/Rockefeller ticket so I basically had to wait for
four years for the opportunity to get even with him for the
Martin roast. And I did, starting in 1978 at a USO event:

Ronald Reagan still has visions of the White House, but time is running out on him—nobody's hair stays that color forever.

In fact, I was happy when I first heard Ronald Reagan was running for the presidency. I've always thought, once you're in show business you should stay in it.

...and in my TV monologue, October 1978:

Incidentally, I want to announce that I'm not a candidate. That's funny, Ronnie Reagan usually gets big laughs with that line....Hey, but this is an election year. And you can always tell when elections are on TV. You start to appreciate the regular commercials. It's this time of year that you know why they call it the "boob tube."

...and Christmas 1979 on NBC:

Some people are claiming that Ronald Reagan is too old to be president of the United States. But I like Ronnie. He's smart, he's honest and he's the only candidate who calls me "sonny."...Ronnie is going around the country making lots of speeches and I hear Congress is furious. They wish he'd stop referring to them as "extras."

By the time election year 1980 came around, everyone was fair game:

...Among Republicans, Reagan is out in front, although no other prominent Republican has endorsed him. That figures—they're all running.

...Reagan's defeat by George Bush in the Iowa primary is very biblical. It's only the second time in history someone received a message from a bush.

...Ted Kennedy's appearing on TV every chance he gets. The other night he was pin boy on "Bowling for Dollars."

...Just in case the Fords do move back into the White House, Betty wrote Dear Abby for tips on how to remove grits from tablecloths.

...Carter decided to start campaigning when he called his election headquarters and Joan Kennedy answered the phone. However, Billy helped—he didn't say anything.

...Jerry Brown returned to Sacramento to find out that while he was campaigning [Lieutenant Governor] Mike Curb appointed another governor.

...John Anderson decided to run as an Independent and has already suggested how to choose the winner. He wants to do it alphabetically.

But it narrowed down to Reagan and Bush versus Carter and Mondale. I referred to the debates as "The Jimmy and Ronnie Show," also known as "Championship Sniping." It was quite an event: Ultrabrite versus Brylcreem.

Santa arrived early for Ronald Reagan. He woke up one morning with the whole country stuffed in his stocking. I don't know why they even bothered with an inauguration ceremony. But they did, and I was happy to be invited to be part of the gala:

> *...Reagan has been rehearsing for the inaugural all week. He wanted to do it in one take....Nancy had some trouble with him in rehearsing their first dance for the ball. It's not easy to follow a partner who keeps circling to the right.*

The first day in office Reagan added some color and taste to the Oval Office—a jar full of jelly beans to offer his guests. Somehow I expected more of a change than from peanuts to jelly beans.

One day after Reagan took office, the U.S. hostages in Iran were released, following 444 days in captivity. Now I could joke about it at a personal appearance:

> *...They wouldn't let them go until after Ronald Reagan defeated Jimmy Carter in the 1980 election. Not that they were anxious to see Ronnie as president; they were afraid if he didn't get elected, he'd go back to acting.*

Reagan made history his first year in office by: one, appointing Sandra Day O'Connor as the first woman justice on the U.S. Supreme Court:

Damn, I wish I could remember the joke I told Ronald and Nancy. By their reaction I could be getting some laughs with it today.

> *...Now we finally have a woman on the Supreme Court. Ronald Reagan couldn't be happier. Nancy is making breakfast for him again. Nancy is designing a robe for Justice O'Connor. Of course, it'll be basic red.*

...and, two, signing a bill mandating the deepest tax and budget cuts in U.S. history:

He also took on organized labor by firing all the air traffic controllers:

> *..."Hail to the Chief" has been replaced with "Comin' In on a Wing and a Prayer."*

The Reagans had such phenomenal appeal to the public that even the political satirists seemed to soften their criticism. Not that both Ronald and First Lady Nancy didn't have their vulnerabilities. There were plenty: he with his nodding off at Cabinet meetings, a number of aides who were ethically bankrupt, a sagging economy and, always, his age. Phyllis Diller came to his rescue on the age issue by saying, "There is an advantage to a president's being over 70. At least he doesn't have to listen to his mother." And Nancy, too, who seemingly had an air of aristocracy in her taste for designer clothes and exquisitely catered affairs. She also consulted with an astrologer.

It may have been their charm and general likability that prompted the congresswoman from Colorado, Pat Schroeder, to label the Reagan presidency as the "Teflon presidency"—no matter what went wrong, nothing seemed to stick to Reagan. But a hallmark of the Reagan presidency was humor. The Reagans laughed at themselves. It was President Reagan who set the tone of humor after his assassination attempt. Upon entering the hospital he wanted to know if his doctors were Republicans. And no one laughed harder than the first lady when she heard the joke:

When Nancy was asked her opinion of Red China, she answered, "It's terrible, just terrible. It will clash with the drapes in the White House dining room."

The presidential campaign of 1984 was between Ronnie Reagan and Walter Mondale. They scheduled a big TV debate, and it certainly stirred up a lot of interest—and monologue jokes:

...Ronnie's advisers are afraid that Reagan will fall asleep while Mondale is talking. Or worse, while he's talking....The two candidates have started fighting about who is more religious. Mondale got a little nervous when he saw skywriting that said: REAGAN IN '84. There was no plane. Just a giant finger.

There was only one thing wrong with having President Reagan on my TV special—he wanted his name above the title.

Ronnie and George Bush won the election easily, which is something of an understatement. Mondale and his veep candidate, Geraldine Ferraro, carried only one state, Minnesota. Ronnie would have carried that one, too, but nobody told him it was there.

Reagan topped all my jokes that year, making up one of his own. Testing the microphone for his weekly radio broadcast, he said, "My fellow Americans, I'm pleased to tell you today that I've signed legislation that will outlaw Russia forever. We begin bombing in five minutes."

Somehow, the joke got on the air. If it had been Orson Welles who said it, it would have caused a national panic. But since is was Reagan, nobody took it seriously. They just figured Nancy had forgotten to make out his cue cards.

The fact that I used to call the White House before every special was taped to tell my material to Reagan was brought out in a press interview in 1985:

> *"Does the president ever ask you to eliminate any of your stories?" I was asked. "No way," I replied. "Even if he doesn't like them, he'll give you a smile anyway. Besides, Reagan never fires anybody. He promotes them."*

The prez had a chance to get back into show business with a surprise visit to my two-hour birthday special in May 1987. We stood toe-to-toe on an outdoor stage at Pope Air Force Base in North Carolina and traded one-liners. At one point during the banter we pointed fingers at each other and simultaneously said, "I hope I look that good when I'm your age."

During the uproar, I commented to the president, "When vaudeville comes back, we're ready—we'll flip for top billing." I was told afterward that when the president decided to surprise me he told aides not to worry about a script. "Bob and I are old pals. We'll throw something together." And we did:

> *I told him that since the crowd had started gathering at 10 o'clock in the morning that I thought for this particular audience of paratroopers he might "drop in by parachute."*

He replied, "Bob, I leave that to the experts. I probably would land in the middle of your birthday cake."

"Yeah," I said, "we wouldn't want icing all over the seat of power. Gee, it's been great having you. I'm sorry Nancy isn't along."

Borrowing the motto of the first lady's war on drugs, Reagan replied, "Well, Bob, I was going to ask her, but I was afraid she'd 'just say no.'"

Dear Bob — What was that tag line again?
Warm Regard Ron

In 1987 Reagan's famous quotes "Well, there they go again!" and "Have some jelly beans" finally made room for more serious words when he stood at the Brandenburg Gate with his back to the Berlin Wall and shouted, "Mr.

Gorbachev, open this gate! Mr. Gorbachev, tear down this wall." Rumor has it that Reagan was so startled when it actually happened in 1989, as predicted by Nancy's astrologer, that he called her and asked her to put two dollars for him on a horse in the Kentucky Derby.

Gorbachev asked for a meeting before Reagan left office. According to my monologues:

Reagan has been offered more than five million dollars for his autobiography. Gorbachev has written his and is only getting 14 rubles for it. Gorby has asked for a summit meeting with Reagan to find out the name of his literary agent.

Their meetings made history. Reagan was the actor, but Gorby upstaged him every time. I went on the air with:

Gorbachev started his visit by stopping his limo in Washington so he could shake hands with the spectators. He was the first leader of a country to hold out his hand in our nation's capital and not come away with foreign aid....It was easy to spot Gorbachev. His limo had a bumper sticker saying I BRAKE FOR REPORTERS. *Everything Reagan does, Gorbachev does him one better. Reagan wears the flag of his country in his lapel. Gorby wears the map of his country on his forehead.*

We all felt that this was the beginning of the end of the Cold War. Things were looking so rosy, I even traded in my Kaopectate jokes.

Reagan left the White House with the highest rating since FDR. He was as popular with Americans as prune juice was with the "Golden Girls." I thought Ronnie might return to making pictures. After all, he still had some makeup left. But he retired to work on his golf game. All his shots still go to the right, by the way.

Dolores and I have known Ronald and Nancy for a long time: when he was an actor, president of the Screen Actors Guild, governor of California and president of the United States. It's not his fault he could never hold a job.

What a Treat for an Actor, Seeing His Name on the Front Page of the Newspaper Nearly Every Day

One of my favorite routines surrounded the sad occasion of Anwar Sadat's funeral in October 1981. To represent the United States, President Reagan asked three former presidents—Richard Nixon, Gerald Ford and Jimmy Carter—to fly to Egypt on Air Force One:

We had three ex-presidents on Air Force One....
I don't know how airlines do it. They were put on
Air Force One and somehow their luggage was put
on Air Force Two.

Ronnie saw them off. It's always a great feeling to
take three politicians and ship them off to another
land.

They all fought over who got the seat of honor. They
finally gave it to the pilot.

Everything was fine except for one little thing—the
Democrat kept trying to get into first class. You
could tell it was a Republican plane—only Jimmy
Carter felt any turbulence.

When we returned home from our 1968 Christmas overseas tour for the GIs, actor-turned Governor Reagan met us at the airport. He was not running for president then...or so he kept telling everybody every chance he got. With us on the platform is Les Brown and Ann-Margret.

There was an awkward moment for the Republicans when they flew over Mount Rushmore. They glanced down and realized they were outnumbered.

It was a movie flight, but all of them had already seen **Bedtime for Bonzo.**

At first they didn't want to just sit around and talk. They did that while they were in office. But they talked for practically the whole flight. They're still politicians, you know.

They talked together for about three hours. Then they each got about a half hour for rebuttal. It might have been the greatest debate of all time, and none of them running for office.

They had to talk politics. That's all they have in common. It was either that or, "How's the peanut crop this year?"

President Reagan hates making budget cuts:

...But he had no choice. He got all choked up when he had to tell Lee Iacocca, "Sorry, no more food stamps."

...And to set an example, he's been making sacrifices, too. Did you know he's now buying day-old jelly beans?

...And some of his Reaganomics took real courage. Like when he said to Nancy, "I hate to tell you this, but we're going to have to make do with the same old tablecloths."

Reagan's Kitchen Cabinet has it own troubles:

Budget director David Stockton blabbed that Reagan's economic program was designed to help the rich. Well, if the Republicans won't help them, who will?

Secretary of State Alexander Haig, Secretary of Defense Caspar Weinberger and National Security Adviser Richard Allen are all feuding. At Cabinet breakfasts all they put out are butter knives.

Can you believe we have an actor in the White House?

Nancy Reagan is no longer considered the first lady. Now she's the leading lady.

George Bush is no longer the vice president. Now he's called the understudy.

And Reagan's the first president to install an applause sign in the Oval Office.

Reagan takes on the Russians:

Both Reagan and Alexander Haig have been talking tough to the Russians....And they're ready for any retaliation. Every time the Cabinet meets, they put their limousines in a circle.

Reagan said the Russians would lie and cheat to attain their objectives. I didn't know they had elections.

People are talking—Reagan gets a hearing aid:

Did you see that President Reagan finally got a hearing aid? People have been telling Reagan to get one for years—but he couldn't hear them.

When the doctors examined his ear they were surprised to find nerve damage. They thought it might just be a jelly bean stuck in there.

He only wears it in his right ear because he doesn't want to hear from the left.

Shades of *Casablanca*—"Ronnie, this looks like the start of a beautiful friendship."

I knew he was having trouble hearing when he was looking at his watch and I asked him, "What time is it?" And he answered, "Bulova."

Actually, it was Congress who talked him into getting it. They've been telling him to stick it in his ear for years.

GEORGE HERBERT WALKER BUSH

It's so cold here in Washington, D.C., that politicians have their hands in their own pockets.

Thank you, ladies and gentlemen, thank you. Yessir, this is Bob Hope, starting my 39th year on NBC, telling you I've got four new writers with me, and I know their jokes can't fail. You may have heard their names before: Dukakis, Bentsen, Bush and Quayle.

SO WENT THE OPENING for my September 1988 special. It was "open season" on all the voters again. The season started early with Senator Gary Hart throwing his hat in the ring for the Democratic presidential nomination. Then he remembered where he had left his hat. His wife was not amused. And evangelist Pat Robertson threw

George and I reading each other's lips in the backyard of my home in Toluca Lake.

his halo in the ring. But it boiled down to Massachusetts Governor Michael Dukakis and Lloyd Bentsen of Texas challenging Vice President George Bush and Dan Quayle (Dan Quayle???). The good news of the year was that the Dodgers won the World Series, thanks largely to the great pitching of Orel Hershiser.

It was no surprise to anyone that I jumped on the Bush bandwagon early in the game. George and Barbara Bush were like family. I knew his father, Prescott, and played golf with him. During his eight years as Reagan's vice president, I became very close to George and I played a lot of golf with him, too.

One week after my NBC special, I had the honor of introducing Bush at the Republicans' Victory '88 dinner in downtown Los Angeles. After elaborating on his gold-plated credentials to be president of the United States, I tested the Bush sense of humor with a few one-liners:

...George was brought up to be a politician. Before he learned how to crawl, he already knew how to shake hands.

...At age two, George said his first words: "How am I doing in the polls?"

...When Dukakis was a boy, he lived in a poor neighborhood. When George was a boy, his father showed him a picture of one.

I commented on his family home is Kennebunkport, saying that the town was so reclusive that...

...the school song is about another town....Instead of "go" and "stop" signs, theirs say "go" and "keep going."...And when they have a garage sale there, you can buy garages.

On October 27 the Victory '88 campaign fund-raiser came to Toluca Lake where Dolores and I opened our home for a reception honoring George and Barbara Bush. I was heartened to see so many Hollywood celebrities turn out for the event. I didn't realize there were so many committed Republicans in the industry. And when I say committed, I mean it. I was the only freeloader in the bunch. Dolores took care of all the details, save one.

My contribution to the event was creating a large sign that extended halfway across the back of the house, which read, WELCOME "OREL" BUSH. I had to explain that damn sign to everyone who came to the event. Everyone but George Bush. He smiled; he liked it. Then again, behind the smile he may have been saying to himself, "All these years we've known one another and Bob still doesn't know my first name."

Missing from the event was the vice-presidential candidate, Dan Quayle. A story went around that he had missed Air Force One because he couldn't remember the flight number.

Bush and Quayle easily won the election and Bush got off to a good start. Within two weeks Rich Little was impersonating him.

Bob— will the two people in blue please not stand next to each other! Geo. Bush

By the time you get to meet 10 presidents you would think that you'd find at least two who had the same approach to humor. No way. For starters, I would define the Bush sense of humor as refined. He has a warm, not raucous, but most genuine laugh. He jokes but he's a better listener than a "teller," which to a comedian makes him a great audience. He is a very secure man and consequently he doesn't take himself too seriously. Political satirists, impersonators and especially cartoonists had their way with him, but the thrust of their ridicule focused in on Vice President Dan Quayle. Finally, a vice president who didn't get lost in the system—they wouldn't let him. We had a vice president who soon became a household word. I wasn't sure what that word was—but he was known. Dan Quayle, vice president at 41 years of age. I've got golf balls older than that.

Before he even took office, George Bush had uttered two of his famous quotes. One was, "I hate broccoli." And when he was asked if, as president, he would raise taxes, he said, "No." When asked again, he repeated, "No." When asked yet again, he was somewhat exasperated and said, "Read my lips—no new taxes."

During my Christmas monologue in 1988 I had a chance to comment about that quote:

> *George Bush will soon be sworn in, but I still have to come to grips with whether he'll repeat the oath or we'll have to read his lips.*

> *You know, George Bush had an image problem: Before the convention, people thought he was such a wimp, the polo player on his shirt rode sidesaddle.... I said to Bush, "It's a miracle that you're so much better than you were before." He said, "I think the same thing about you, whenever you're funny."*

On the day following the Bush inauguration I reported on the event in my TV monologue:

> *Bush and Quayle have been sworn in, and the country will do just fine. But I still can't picture Reagan in an unemployment line.*

Did you know that George Bush, our new president, is a fisherman, a hunter, plays tennis and, at Yale, played baseball and football? He's so sports-minded that after the inauguration yesterday, when he swore on the Bible, he went inside and swore again on the **Sporting News.** *Talk about being an athlete. Bush will be the first president to greet foreign leaders with a high five.*

Bush loves to tell our story about one of his fishing trips:

"I don't know if people remember this or not, but I went on a fishing trip in Maine and got a hook from my son Jeb's line caught in my ear. Bob was ready with the one-liners. He said, 'It was a good fishing trip, though. They caught 14 trout, eight bass and one ear.' Then Bob said, 'The president didn't have to go to the hospital. They just took the hook out, weighed him and threw him back.' Then he added, 'But they immediately notified Dan Quayle. After all, he is only an earlobe away from the Oval Office.'"

I add the final one-liners...

...I was surprised that Jeb hooked his dad. He was using broccoli for bait.

The number-one laugh topic on my personal appearance tours across the country in 1989 was the George Bush administration and the Bush White House:

Vice President Bush had a couple of tickets for the 1981 All Star Game in Cleveland and took me along.

San Diego (January)

...Did you see all the Bush kids and grandkids at the inauguration? They may turn the White House into a day-care center. Did you see the picture of President Bush reading a fairy tale to his grandchildren? I think it was called the Federal Budget.

Miami (February)

...Bush is in Colombia this week for a summit meeting with all the world leaders. It's a scary situation down there. They began the summit with a prayer. It lasted for five hours.

Las Vegas (March)

*...The **L.A.** **Times** gave George Bush a "C" on his first 100 days in office. No one knows what Dan Quayle got. He claims he lost his report card on his way home from the White House.*

Detroit (April)

...The president was criticized for not responding soon enough to the Exxon Valdez crisis. I don't know. I think his idea of using 5 million Q-tips wasn't bad.

Los Angeles (May)

... The president is real serious about reducing air pollution. He wants to clean up our air by the year 2000. I just hope we can hold our breath till then.

Westbury, Long Island (June)

...Did you hear that the first dog, Millie, is writing her memoirs? I understand that one of the titles under consideration is Read My Paws. All this is according to her typist, Barbara Bush.

Norman, Oklahoma (July)

...Did you read that the president is out of the country again? Now it can be told. George Bush never wanted the presidency—all he wanted were the frequent flyer miles.

Rochester, Minnesota (August)

...Did you see President Bush golfing this past week? He likes to play once in a while. It gives him a chance to swear at something other than Congress.

Paducah, Kentucky (September)

...George Bush went for 18 days on his vacation without catching a fish. I didn't know that many bass were Democrats.

New York City (October)

George Bush is declaring war on drugs. Let's hope he has more luck catching the drug dealers than he has had catching fish.

Orlando, Florida (November)

...As you know, horseshoes is a favorite game of the Bush family. However, I think the president has an uphill battle in trying to make the sport our national pastime.

From NBC, Burbank (December)

...I hear that Santa is going to bring something to President Bush that he's had trouble getting all year—a fish. Santa made an early visit to the White House. All 11 Bush grandkids were there, and there was a lot of pushing and shoving to see who could talk to Santa first. Finally, Barbara Bush stepped in and told Dan Quayle that he would have to wait his turn.

For the most part, President Bush was receiving good grades for his management of foreign affairs. The Berlin Wall came down and the Soviet Union and Eastern Europe were embracing democracy:

...Before giving his State of the Union speech, President Bush called Gorbachev. But the Soviet leader couldn't talk long. He was afraid that he would lose his place in line at McDonald's.

In his fight to control drug traffic from South America he sent military forces to Panama that overthrew the

Bob Friendship 6·20·89

government and captured military strongman General Manuel Noriega, who we punished by putting him up in comfortable quarters in Miami Beach. But Bush's domestic policies were in trouble. For one thing he declared war on all the broccoli growers:

> *I warned him, don't anger the broccoli growers. If there's anybody better than politicians at tossing manure around, it's farmers.*

In the fall of 1990 all hell broke loose on the international front when the Iranian funny man, Saddam Hussein, decided to annex Kuwait. The United Nations came down on his head but he refused to yield and pull his troops out of Kuwait. President Bush acted swiftly and deftly to establish, for the United Nations, a NATO-united armed force in ready-alert in Saudi Arabia. It was called "Operation Desert Shield."

Once again our men and women in uniform were

being called upon to serve. President Bush had spent Thanksgiving with them; I wanted to spend Christmas. I called the president and suggested we do a show for those serving in Operation Desert Shield at Christmastime. Others were going over on handshaking tours, but I wanted to do a show.

The president called Secretary of Defense Dick Cheney and said, "Give Bob Hope whatever he wants." In turn, Dick Cheney called me and said, "The president said to give you whatever you want. What do you want?" I answered, "A C-141 and permission to entertain the troops in Saudi Arabia." That Christmas Dolores and I, along with Ann Jillian, Marie Osmond, the Pointer Sisters, Aaron Tippin, Khrystyne Haje and Johnny Bench, were perspiring and performing in Saudi Arabia. As busy as the president must have been in preparing for Operation Desert Storm, he took time out to call us on the plane as we were returning to the States just to say hello and ask how the trip went.

On Easter Sunday 1991 Dolores and I entertained 350 Marines from Twentynine Palms, California, who had returned home from Saudi Arabia, at our home in Palm Springs. The event, "Bob Hope's Yellow Ribbon Party," was taped and aired on NBC. Star billing on the show went to President George Bush, who greeted the guests from Rhode Island via satellite:

HOPE: Mr. President. I haven't talked to you since you called us on the plane on our way home from Saudi Arabia.

PRESIDENT BUSH: It's the only place I knew where to reach you. Christmastime on a plane coming back from seeing the troops, or on the golf course.

HOPE: Please, never call me on the golf course.

PRESIDENT BUSH: Look, I promise. Now, how many Christmases have you spent with the Armed Forces in the last 43 years?

HOPE: Oh, lots of them, and we loved every minute of it.

PRESIDENT BUSH: Well, I know it means a great deal to them and always has. You've boosted the morale of our troops from World War II to Desert Storm, and I remember when you first started this at March Field.

HOPE: Really! You remember that?

PRESIDENT BUSH: Yes, I was in the third grade at the time.

Operation Desert Storm began on February 24, 1991, and ended in 100 hours with Iraqi forces defeated. National polls gave Bush the highest approval rating of a president since Franklin Roosevelt.

(April 1991 monologue)

President Bush did everything he said he was going to do. It's a whole new concept in politics. His popularity is so high now that he can leave politics and become a rock star.

In May 1992 we went to Columbus, Ohio, to tape my TV special at the international floral and garden show, AmeriFlora '92. It was a beautiful and classy venue and we wanted some classy stars. It just happened that Barbara Bush was the honorary patron of AmeriFlora and would appear on the show. You can't get a bigger marquee name than the first lady of the land. I interviewed Barbara in a beautiful garden setting. I told her how happy we were that she could take time out of her busy schedule to join us on the show and that:

...I was in a bookstore the other day checking on Millie's book, and I tell you, it was really crowded. I had a tough time getting a copy of it; in fact, I had to stand in line behind two poodles and a Pomeranian.

Between Frank Sinatra with his hand shadows and Barbara Bush making "donkey ears'" over George Schlatter's head, the photographer had a hard time getting a decent group shot of the cast at the "USO Welcome Home Desert Storm" taping at Universal Studios in April 1991. President Bush groupies included: Tony Danza, Brooke Shields, Victoria Tennant, the Pointer Sisters (June and Ruth shown), Tom Selleck, Arnold Schwarzenegger and James Woods.

She informed me that all the money from the sales of the book would go to charity and that it would be out in paperback in the late summer, and it's in German and Japanese now....The Japanese version must be great; you buy two books, you get egg roll.

What a wonderful guest. She gave me all the funny lines. George was there, too, but was very careful not to upstage his wife...or me, as a matter of fact. What a gentleman.

While Bush and Quayle were on their Victory '92 campaign trail to stave off the Clinton/Gore challenge, Dolores and I were planning another reception for the president in our backyard. This time there were no clever

And there's another one about Dan Quayle that goes...

signs, just signs that read: LADIES, GENTLEMEN AND DEMO-CRATS. I started my introduction of the president by saying:

...We were going to put Congress in charge of serving dinner tonight but we were afraid nothing would ever get passed.

...I even golfed with his father. He's the only president I can say that about. All Lincoln's dad and I ever did was a little lawn bowling.

I joined President Bush in Houston, Texas, on the Monday night before Election Day. At the "Welcome Home, George Bush" rally there, I got a chance to finish my introduction, which concluded:

...Ladies and gentlemen, I'm honored to present the president of the United States, George Bush.

162 DEAR PREZ, I WANNA TELL YA!

And in an aside to him:

Okay, Prez? Now, let's play golf.

President George Bush—Read His Quips

George Bush, Family Man:

George Bush is family-oriented, fair and decent. Now we know what it's like to have Ward Cleaver as president of the United States.

The Bushes have brought a homey atmosphere to the White House with the family dog, children and grandchildren all over the place. I tried to call the president last week and they said he doesn't take phone calls during recess.

There are so many children that a top-secret document is now considered anything that doesn't have jelly-stained fingerprints on it.

Bush addresses the deficit problem:

He has a brilliant plan: He'll let the Japanese buy the entire country, and then it'll be their problem.

George Bush's run for re-election in '92:

And he has all his ducks in a row—and one Quayle.

He's also announced that Barbara will be his wife again for the next election. The announcement made a lot of people very happy—mostly comedy writers.

Bush confronts hecklers at a fund-raiser:

The hecklers who infiltrated the president's fund-raising dinner had to pay a thousand dollars to get in. So much for free speech.

The Washington press corps was outraged that Bush was treated so badly by hecklers. That's their job.

Don't people know that they don't have to heckle the president of the United States? That's what Congress is for.

I was at a dinner recently with the president. The hecklers were really mad at him. They booed him during my jokes.

George Bush is a great golfer:

I know nobody else who yells, "Read my scorecard."

...But it's hard to play in the foursome ahead of him. He doesn't yell "Fore." He just says, "Read my lips."

The president's new space program:

President Bush wants to launch an expensive space program to search for signs of intelligent life in the universe. Maybe they should start searching for some in Washington.

He also wants to send men to Mars. Most of those men are Democrats, but...

Bush is traveling so much he may develop a Cabinet post for his travel agent:

President Bush is on the road again—Saudi Arabia, Egypt, Europe, Mexico. It's amazing the lengths he'll go to get away from broccoli.

Bush knew it would be rough drumming up support for his Persian Gulf policies, but I don't think he realized that he'd have to go door to door.

He's traveled so much it appears that he's using the White House as a pit stop.

It's open season on Quayle—and you don't even need a hunting license:

Can you believe what's happening to Dan Quayle— our punching bag-elect?

Some people say he got the nomination just because he's young and handsome. That's why I thought I was going to get it.

I know Quayle doesn't sound very authoritative now, but just wait until his voice changes.

During the election they're really keeping Quayle away from the public. The only time you can see his face in Washington is on the side of a milk carton.

No, Dan Quayle is a very astute fund-raiser. A good speller, no, but a great fund-raiser. Quayle called Bush and said, "Sir, I'm having a problem with the inauguration." And George said, "You mean deciding what you are going to say?" And Quayle said, "No...getting invited to it."

The media has really been after Quayle. That's unprecedented in American politics. No one usually pays that much attention to a vice president. Vice president—that's a square peg in an Oval Office. On the ship of state the vice president is a dinghy.

How about Dan Quayle attacking TV's Murphy Brown? Murphy had a baby, and Quayle had a fit. Quayle says that Murphy's baby was illegitimate, in so many words. Murphy Brown said pretty much the same thing about Quayle.

I'm not saying Dan Quayle is young, but he's probably the first politician to hold a national office who knows all the words to Madonna's records.

All the Quayle jokes won't hinder him from doing his job—just as soon as he figures out what that is.

Quayle thinks "Roe vs. Wade" are two ways to cross the Potomac.

BILL (WILLIAM JEFFERSON) CLINTON

Personally, I'm for foreign aid. And the sooner we get it, the better.

TO ME, BILL CLINTON entered show business on November 10, 1979, when he did a walk-on during my show at the University of Arkansas in Fayetteville. He happened to be in his first term as the governor of Arkansas. He shared the spotlight with me again in Little Rock during his third term as governor in July 1984. Let me tell you, watching him work the crowd both times, this man was all show biz. He had to be on the stage, or, at least in the White House.

Seven years later to the day, July 4, 1991, I found myself riding in a car to the governor's mansion to attend a reception hosted by Mrs. Clinton. I was there for the Hope of America Stadium Show benefiting the Children's Miracle Network (CMN), of which I was national chairman and Hillary Rodham Clinton was the Arkansas chairman. There was somewhat of an obligation to attend the party being held to honor the National Guard troops that had been activated for Operation Desert Storm. I mumbled and grumbled to Joe Lake, co-founder of CMN, who was riding with me: "Why is a good Republican boy like me doing 15 minutes of material in a Democratic governor's living room? I just hope that George Bush doesn't get wind of this."

On the way back to the hotel I made a prediction to Joe: "Bill Clinton will be the next president of the United States." On that Wednesday morning in November 1992, I phoned Joe, yelled "I TOLD YOU SO!" and hung up.

The 1992 presidential campaign started early. Then again, they always do, about three years too early. Although Pat Buchanan was out in full force with his conservative agenda it was certain the incumbents Bush and Quayle were shoo-ins to become the nominees of the Republican party. But there were some new faces on the scene: Democrats Bill Clinton and Senator Al Gore Jr. of Tennessee, and computer software executive Ross Perot, who headed the Reform Party, a strong grassroots political organization.

The major issues of that election year were the struggling national economy, health care and Ross Perot's haircut. For me, poking fun at the presidential hopefuls started with my March 1992 monologue:

> *...Well, the election campaign in the country is picking up speed. The voters are yawning faster....All the candidates are talking about health care now. Don't they realize that it's their campaign speeches that make us sick?...You know, we could wipe out the federal deficit if there was a tax on campaign promises.*

September 3, 1995 at the Waikiki Shell, Kapiolani Park, Hawaii, for a World War II Commemorative Service—President Clinton, Dolores, Maxene Andrews, yours truly and Hillary Rodham Clinton sang "America, The Beautiful."

...All the candidates are coming to California. Clinton is trying to convince Californians that he's one of them. Yesterday, he held a press conference while hangin' ten in the surf off Malibu.

Clinton's image was strong but often mixed. To some he was a five-term governor who was comfortable sitting on a tractor. Others knew him as a graduate of Yale Law School and a Rhodes scholar, who was also a teacher and a state attorney general. Still others saw the image of a liberal who allegedly smoked pot in the '60s. Clinton put these critics in their place when he made his famous president-elect quote, "But I didn't inhale."

Clinton had an infectious smile a la Franklin Roosevelt,

"Three presidents and a duffer." At the 1995 Desert Classic, Clinton had the longest drive, Ford the best scores and Bush the most hits....I had the most erasures on a scorecard.

the charm of Jimmy Carter, and Ronald Reagan's ability to romance an audience, be it in person or on television. He was either a conservative liberal or a liberal conservative who was trying to pull the Democratic party toward the center. Will the real Bill Clinton please stand up?

Al Gore, Clinton's running mate, was a strong environmentalist who had all the qualities of most vice presidents—while they're vice presidents. Need I elaborate?

The fight for the presidency was a rather bitter one. But the winner, in the south-left corner wearing red, white and blue jogging shorts, was Bill Clinton. The Clinton/Gore ticket won 43 percent of the popular vote over 38 percent for Bush/Quayle. The deciding factor in the election was Ross Perot, who pulled in a surprising 19 percent of the popular vote.

We had the first musician in the White House since Truman, and I had a chance to put it in rhyme in my

November 1992 monologue…

Clinton's going to Washington,
Arkansas folks are thrilled to the core.
They won't have to hear him practice
on that saxophone anymore.

…Having a saxophone player in the White House
could be interesting. He may not pull us out of the
recession, but while the country is singing the blues,
he can play along.

…Now that Clinton has made an elephant
disappear, maybe he can do the same thing with
the deficit.

…We're losing a president who tosses horseshoes
and gaining one who could probably put them on
a horse. Bill Clinton could be the first president
sworn in at the inaugural wearing a top hat with
"John Deere" written on it.

…All of the pictures of Lincoln and Roosevelt in the
Oval Office are rejected now. They've been replaced
with pictures of Homer and Jethro.

…President Clinton is looking forward to entertain-
ing leaders from other countries. I just hope Boris
Yeltsin likes okra and catfish.

With Christmas approaching, my writers and I were
still caught up in the excitement of yet another president
making his ascent to the White House:

It's a different type of Christmas in Washington this year. You can tell there's a Christmas on Capitol Hill. The Nativity scene is on the lawn in front of Congress, and the three wise men all have Arkansas accents.

...And the way Bill Clinton plays the saxophone, he's not selecting a Cabinet, he's looking for sidemen. Leave it to a politician to be good at playing a wind instrument. He may have the first Cabinet in history with a rhythm section.

...Bill Clinton has spent a lot of time jogging around Washington. I'm not saying he doesn't look too good in his jogging shorts, but the Lincoln statue has its hands over its eyes.

...Y'know, the Clintons may have to take a bus to the inauguration. The Bush administration hasn't returned the presidential limo yet. Bill Clinton taking a bus to the inauguration isn't bad. The alternative is his driving a tractor.

...Clinton loves to make long speeches. In fact, this will be the first inaugural address with an intermission.

...The Clintons will have an open house. That means anyone can get in, even Republicans. The Clintons wanted to invite the public into their new home, but Hillary said, "They can come in, but I'm not going to bake anything for them."
...I'm a little suspicious of the invitation. I think they just want us to help them unpack.

...The Democrats want everybody to come and visit the White House. They never know when they'll get the chance again.

In May of 1993, Dolores and I were staying at the Waldorf Towers in New York when there was a knock on the door. Rarely are both of us speechless at the same time, but when you open a door and see the president of the United States looking at you, smiling and saying, "I was in the neighborhood and thought I'd stop in to say hello"...words don't come easy. What a pleasure and what an honor, and to this day, neither one of us remembers what we said to President Clinton.

With this kind of laugh, President Clinton has the inside track to capture the comedian vote. The occasion was the Medal of Arts presentations on the South Lawn of The White House in October1995.

Birthdays are important. Some people spend them quietly. Me, I make a television special out of them. That's why I have not been able to lie about my age for so many years. My daughter Linda surprised me several years ago when we were at home watching my latest special, and

The Prez liked my joke...but, Dolores, God bless her, loved it.

there was President Clinton on my show, wishing me a happy birthday and issuing an invitation: "And the next time you're in Washington I'd like to ask you to stop by the White House. Frankly, I need some advice. For starters, I need some help with my back swing. More important, if, like me, you have to spend this much time in the capital, I need your gift of laughter."

When the 1995 Bob Hope Chrysler Classic in Palm Springs came around, there were two presidents scheduled to play in the golf tournament, Jerry Ford and George Bush. *Wouldn't it be great*, I thought to myself, *if we could break a record at the Classic and have three presidents in one foursome?* So I asked President Clinton to join us and he said yes. We billed ourselves as "three presidents and a duffer." And what a time we had: Clinton had the longest drive, Ford had the best score and Bush the most hits. (It appears that while we weren't looking, Bush had taken a golfing lesson from Ford.) I was the winner of the day. Look at the foursome I got to play in.

Evidently, President Clinton wanted a chance to get the money I owed him during the play in Palm Springs so in May, he invited me to play with him at the Army/Navy Golf Course in Washington, D.C. He got even—he beat me again. Do you have any idea how hard it is to fudge on your scorecard with all those Secret Service men looking over your shoulder? But I got even with him. I forgot to pay him.

Both Dolores and I were honored to share several stages with President and Hillary Clinton in September 1995 in Hawaii for the 50th anniversary commemoration of the end of World War II. Many fond and sad memories were rekindled during the week of ceremony; and many new memories created in a renewed acquaintance with the Clintons.

In less than 30 days, Dolores and I were at the White House. It appears that in a moment of weakness the National Endowment for the Arts added me to the roster of individuals to be honored. Hosted by the president and first lady, the ceremony took place on the East Lawn of the White House, where that night we were guests at a black tie dinner. It was a truly lovely occasion and, contrary to what I have reported, they did not serve grits.

In December of 1995, we taped a special video to be played on Christmas for the men and women in and en route to Bosnia. The response of the recording artists and Hollywood talent was wonderful. But I needed a strong opening act for the show, so I called the prez in Washington and asked, "Are you available?" And he said, "Give me 10 minutes to change ties and put on some makeup," or something like that. Seriously though, Bill Clinton has always been there, ready and willing whenever I've needed him.

The marquee for my 1996 Presidential special on NBC included Ann-Margret, Tony Danza, Don Johnson, Naomi Judd and Tom Selleck, plus David and Julie Eisenhower. But, the top billing went to three presidents and their first ladies, who had a chance to get even—Jerry and Betty Ford, George and Barbara Bush, and Bill and Hillary Clinton. Midnight oil must have been burning at the White House as the Clintons came bearing quips. (Between you and me, I think they had a little help from my writers, Gene Perret and Martha Bolton. Or should I say, *former* writers?)

PRESIDENT CLINTON: One of the perks of being president is that you get to play golf with Bob Hope. And one of the perks of Bob getting to know the presidents is that he can write a book about it.

HILLARY CLINTON: Bob is welcome at the White House anytime.

PRESIDENT CLINTON: He's welcome, but we have started counting the towels.

HILLARY CLINTON: Bob has needled Bill about his saxophone playing, eating at McDonald's, his jogging, his golf. I never realized that Bob Hope and I had so much in common.

And here we are ready for another election. House Majority Leader Bob Dole from Kansas has resigned his

Senate seat to run for the presidency on the Republican ticket. And it appears that President Bill Clinton will be seeking a second term. He really won't make up his mind until the Democratic National Convention. I guess he doesn't want to tip his hand. Then they'll be off and running, and the American public is in for a period of character assassination.

Where else but in America are educated, respected leaders brought down from their pedestals every four years to be mocked, criticized and ridiculed? Then after such a frantic battle, the fist shaking is replaced with handshaking, mockery becomes praise, criticism is quieted, and we put our leaders back on their pedestals for another four years. Well, at least until after the inauguration, anyway.

And where else but in America can a scrawny kid, born in England, raised in Cleveland and educated in vaudeville, grow up and make friends with 11 presidents? It is doubtful that had I stayed in Great Britain I would be playing golf or cracking jokes over a Brandy Alexander with the Queen of England. Let me think about that for a minute….The image is fun to play with.

There's No Business Like "Prez" Business.

Bell ringing for the Clinton inauguration:

Bill Clinton wants bells to ring all over America for his inauguration. He wants bells to ring all day long or until his inauguration speech is over—whichever comes first.

If he wants bells to ring for his inauguration, he should have made Quasimodo his vice president.

Checking out the Clinton presidential handshake at a World War II 50th Anniversary event in Hawaii (September 1995).

I'll promise to ring some bells if he'll promise to stop playing the saxophone.

They're going to bring a replica of the Liberty Bell for Clinton to ring. That's just what we need in Washington—something else that's cracked.

Bill Clinton is one of the first presidents who believes in hog calling as a form of relaxation. The trouble is that too many people confuse his hog calling with his saxophone playing.

Jogging as an official presidential sport:

Bill Clinton likes to jog. That's what we need—a president who can outrun Congress.

Bill Clinton likes to work up a sweat every morning before breakfast. I do, too. With me it's called, "getting out of bed."

I don't mind a president who runs well. It's the IRS agents who scare me....Harry Truman was a walker. Walking is like jogging except slower and in cheaper shoes.

No one has ever accused President Clinton of being a slouch when it comes to food:

Our president likes to eat—anything. He's a Democrat but his appetite is bipartisan.

Bill Clinton loves McDonald's: Big Macs, Egg McMuffins. In fact, he calls Al Gore his vice McPresident.

Clinton and the sin tax:

President Clinton wants to pass a sin tax—which is unnecessary. I've found that after a certain age, sin is taxing enough.

My advice is that if you're caught sinning now, just hold up a sign that says, YOUR TAX DOLLARS AT WORK.

Then there's the one about the White House travel service:

President Clinton fired the White House travel service and replaced them with a travel service run by his cousins from Arkansas. It's called "Air Bubba."

All the stewardesses wear overalls.

Instead of handing out peanuts, they give you a hayseed to chew on.

And the sax plays on:

To relax, President Clinton sometimes plays the saxophone in the White House. And all this time, the neighbors thought Socks, the cat, was in heat. And it should surprise no one that he has chased more mice out of the White House than Socks has. I think it's great. All politicians should play wind instruments. Why let all that good hot air go to waste?

EPILOGUE

BEHIND EVERY GOOD PRESIDENT is a joke or two—and, of course, a good wife, the one who *really* needs a good sense of humor.

All the presidents I've known have had two things in common: a sincere dedication to the American people and a good sense of humor. But the final chapter of this book cannot be written without a tribute to the first ladies of our country. The common bond between them is more than dedication and a sense of humor. Lord knows they've had to have these qualities just to survive the ordeal of living in a house with all the shades up so the eyes of the world can look in.

Each first lady has enhanced the White House with her own distinctive style and grace. Without exception, during the good times and the not-so-good times, their support of their husbands has been unwavering. And each addressed a national cause or two or three that not only provided public awareness but the inspiration for others to serve as well.

But they were not just first ladies. They were also experts in being a mother and wife, designer and hostess, speechgiver and campaigner, counselor and honored guest, not to mention chief cook and bottle washer.

And we all know who ended up taking care of the presidential pets. There were plenty of dogs to walk, feed and groom—a Scottie, beagles, spaniels, setters and retrievers. Barbara Bush had to proofread Millie's book. Hillary's chore for first cat Socks provided a new challenge at the White House. Nancy had the hardest job—Ronnie liked horses.

I'm sure they all had to bite a lip and hold back a tear sometime during their tenure at 1600 Pennsylvania Avenue when they became the brunt of biting humor. My apologies to all if I overstayed my welcome on this account. To their husbands, no!

Here's to the first ladies of our nation. And while I'm at it, here's to the first lady of my house, Dolores, who, if it wasn't for *her* sense of humor, would not have stayed with me for 62 years.

OTHER **BOB HOPE** PRODUCTS AVAILABLE:

VIDEO

"Bob Hope: Memories of World War II"

"Bob Hope Remembers...The European Theatre & D-Day"

AUDIO

"This is Bob "On-The-Air" Hope"/"Somewhere In Time: The Songs & Spirit of WWII" (a double album set with Dolores Hope)

"Hopes for the Holidays" (with Dolores Hope)

"Now and Then" (Dolores Hope)

"That's Love" (Dolores Hope)

For order information, call:
1-800-BOB-HOPE
or write to:
Hope Enterprises, Inc.
P. O. Box 1218
Burbank, CA 91507